The Influential S

The Influential School Leader is a unique, accessible guide for any leader seeking to improve their vision and positively influence school communities in the face of adversity. A successful school today requires a nimble learning environment that is supportive, welcoming, and inspiring for teachers, students, and families. Based on numerous contributions from social and organizational psychology, this book provides a dynamic framework that prepares education stakeholders to examine problems from multiple perspectives and dimensions to create durable solutions. An ideal resource for principals, superintendents, department heads, school psychologists, and other educators in positions of leadership, this expansive toolkit is packed with pragmatic strategies and relatable vignettes.

Craig Murphy is an Associate Professor of School Psychology at William James College, USA. Dr. Murphy also serves as a consultant to numerous school districts in his roles as Clinical Director at Bi-County Collaborative in Walpole, MA, and Executive Director of the Family and Educational Wellness Center in Franklin, MA. He is a nationally certified school psychologist and licensed educational psychologist.

John D'Auria is a core faculty member of the Organizational and Leadership Psychology Department and Director of the Educational Leadership Concentration at William James College, USA. A former math teacher, principal, and super-intendent, Dr. D'Auria currently works as a consultant at Teachers21, where he previously served as President.

The Influential School Leader

Inspiring Teachers, Students, and Families Through Social and Organizational Psychology

Craig Murphy and John D'Auria

Routledge
Taylor & Francis Group

NEW YORK AND LONDON

First published 2021
by Routledge
52 Vanderbilt Avenue, New York, NY 10017

and by Routledge
2 Park Square, Milton Park, Abingdon, Oxon, OX14 4RN

Routledge is an imprint of the Taylor & Francis Group, an informa business

© 2021 Taylor & Francis

The right of Craig Murphy and John D'Auria to be identified as authors of this work has been asserted by them in accordance with sections 77 and 78 of the Copyright, Designs and Patents Act 1988.

Library of Congress Cataloging-in-Publication Data
A catalog record for this title has been requested

ISBN: 978-0-367-37021-3 (hbk)
ISBN: 978-0-367-41511-2 (pbk)
ISBN: 978-0-367-81494-6 (ebk)

Typeset in Palatino
by MPS Limited

To Gran and Papa, lifelong teachers in every sense of
the word

– Craig Murphy

To my grandchildren, Ryan & Kevin O'Connor and
Francis Virgil D'Auria

– John D'Auria

Contents

Meet the Authors

Craig Murphy is a nationally certified school psychologist. He received his Ph.D. and M.S. from Pennsylvania State University, both in school psychology. He is an Associate Professor in the School Psychology Program at William James College (WJC) and also remains an active practitioner as the clinical director for a therapeutic school program at the Bi-County Collaborative (BICO) in Walpole, Massachusetts. Dr. Murphy's research interests include understanding, evaluating, and supporting behavioral/social-emotional functioning in children; bridging the gap between research and practice in school psychology; statistics; and research methodology. His research experiences include securing approximately $3 million in federal grants for developing school-based programming for students with emotional and behavioral challenges, as well as developing social-emotional learning curricula.

Dr. Murphy worked as a school psychologist in the Newton (MA) public schools for 14 years before transitioning to William James College and his current clinical director position at BICO. He spent three of those years as the Principle Investigator of the Elementary and Secondary Counseling Grant, a federally funded research project based on his dissertation and aimed to improve the mental health services and programming throughout the school district. Dr. Murphy is a frequent presenter at regional and national conferences on topics related to students with emotional and behavioral challenges, comprehensive approaches to assessment, systems change, social influence, and school programming.

Finally, Dr. Murphy is the executive director at the Family and Educational Wellness Center (www.fewcenter.com). He founded the organization which specializes in assessment, counseling, and consultation. In his role at the center, Dr. Murphy consults to school districts throughout Massachusetts with a focus on leadership and understanding and supporting students with complicated clinical profiles and multi-stressed family systems.

John D'Auria joined the Organizational and Leadership Psychology Department of William James College in 2018. As a core faculty member, he teaches courses in ethics, consulting skills, and school culture. In 2017, Dr. D'Auria was invited to be a Professor of Practice at the Penn Graduate School of Education Division of Teaching Learning. He currently is a member of Penn's Mid-Career Advisory Board and a mentor and thought partner to graduate students in the Mid-Career Doctoral Program. Prior to his work at Penn, Dr. D'Auria was president of Teachers21 from 2010–2017. Teachers21 is a nonprofit, professional development organization that supports educational reform and improvement efforts across a wide variety of public and private sectors. Under Dr. D'Auria's leadership, Teachers21 provided thousands of educators with opportunities to expand their instructional repertoire and deepen their content knowledge, with a special focus on education leadership. In 2010, Dr. D'Auria was appointed by the Massachusetts Commissioner of Education to a statewide task force to study and develop a new framework for the supervision and evaluation of all educators in Massachusetts. In addition, Dr. D'Auria has worked with leaders across Massachusetts to strengthen practitioners' work around social and emotional learning and was appointed to the Rennie Center Condition of Education Advisory Committee, which seeks to build a more coherent, and research-based, vision of public education in Massachusetts.

Prior to his work at Teachers21, Dr. D'Auria was Superintendent of Schools in Canton, Massachusetts. His educational career has spanned over four decades as a math teacher, guidance counselor, principal, superintendent, and consultant. Dr. D'Auria has advised hundreds of school leaders on how to sharpen the academic focus of school teams, develop a vibrant school culture, and manage conflict in the workplace.

Dr. D'Auria's research focuses on the ways in which the assumptions that people hold about intelligence significantly influence their learning. In 2019 he co-authored, with Jonathan A. Suppovitz and James P. Spillane, Meaningful & Sustainable School Improvement with Distributed Leadership. In 2012, he co-authored *School Systems That Learn* with Dr. Paul Ash (Corwin Press) and is the author of *Ten Lessons in Leadership and Learning* (2010), a resource geared toward new and experienced leaders. Dr. D'Auria authored a curriculum for aspiring school leaders called "The DNA of Leadership," which became a cornerstone for the Leadership Licensure Program sponsored by the Massachusetts School Administrators Association. Additionally, Dr. D'Auria co-authored *How to Bring Vision to School Improvement* (Research for Better Teaching, 1993) with Dr. Jon Saphier. He is a frequent speaker at national and regional educational conferences and has served as an executive coach to a wide variety of educational leaders across the country.

Preface

We have spent the past two years integrating our professional experiences and the myriad of contributions of researchers from both social and organizational psychology to create a framework for educational leadership. It is clear to us that educational leaders need a framework to create systemic change in their schools and school districts. Our framework will provide a strong foundation for school communities encountering unexpected changes that require nimble learning and adaptability. We did not anticipate, however, that our framework would be tested so quickly by so many during the three remaining months of the 2019–2020 academic year due to two historic events—the COVID-19 pandemic and the George Floyd murder—both of which (a) presented significant challenges to educational leaders, (b) provided little empirical support to serve as blueprints to inform their responses, and (c) occured during a time period that demands immediate change. Although the goal of this book has always been to inspire educational leaders and increase their influence to improve schools and, ultimately, the education that children receive, the spring of 2020 proves just how valuable effective leadership can be, not only in schools but across the nation.

March 2020 saw the widespread closure of schools due to the COVID-19 pandemic. As time passed and the duration of this crisis stretched from two weeks to a month to two months to the rest of the school year, it became apparent to all educators, students, and families that schools would have to adapt rapidly to distance learning. Students and families waited, some patiently and others not, to hear from teachers and principals about what would happen next. Teachers and principals waited for school administrators to provide guidance. They, in turn, waited for officials at the state level to establish new policies and frameworks for learning. Officials at the state level looked to the federal government for guidance. Collectively, we listened intently to every word spoken by Dr. Anthony Fauci, the Director of the National Institute of Allergy and Infectious Diseases. It has been a scary and unprecedented time for our nation, and schools are once again on the front lines struggling to adapt to the "new normal."

Schools, of course, have done this before, most notably in the 1950s following the Brown v. Board of Education ruling that outlawed racial segregation in schools. The Supreme Court's decision was unanimous, but the process of desegregating schools took decades. Many would argue that a majority of schools are segregated to this day. At the surface level, desegregating American schools should not have been a daunting challenge. Unfortunately, solving complex problems demands looking beneath the surface. The Supreme Court's ruling triggered intense emotions and feelings across the nation. Understanding and managing intense emotional reactions is a difficult process that often hinders our ability to find solutions to complex problems. On top of that, social, political, and geographical systems play a critical role in sustaining flawed practices or ushering in new, more equitable solutions.

Similarly, schools were again on the front lines in 1975 when Public Law 94-142 guaranteed a Free and Appropriate Public Education (FAPE) to millions of children with disabilities. Schools were forced to evaluate how they could differentiate instruction to meet the needs of all children. Preschool programs, early identification practices, and numerous procedural safeguards and protections followed to protect the rights of all students and their families. Individualized Educational Programs (IEPs) were developed for students with disabilities, and evaluation practices were established to inform interventions and monitor progress. Finally, professional development for teachers, many of whom were not prepared to meet the needs of students with disabilities, dramatically changed in an attempt to increase teaching capacity within districts. Collectively, the demands on schools to educate all children, regardless of their challenges or disabilities, clearly required a change at the "systems" level.

Schools continued to be on the front lines following mass shootings at Columbine High School (1999) and Sandy Hook Elementary School (2012), among others. Horrified by these tragedies, we continue today to debate the role schools should play in ensuring student safety. Difficult and tense discussions about metal detectors, firearm safety and rights, evacuation protocols, police officers on school grounds, and even arming classroom teachers continue to this day.

Historical events have forced educational leaders over the past several decades to reconsider their approaches to education and redefine the ways their systems function—often without clear guidance. Although the challenges were well-defined at the surface-level, intense emotions and feelings from each stakeholder group were clearly present beneath the surface, which makes it difficult to respond effectively. Times like these demand that educational leaders accurately diagnose the problem, take the time necessary to see the problem from multiple perspectives, and exert their influence to effect change at the systemic level. These challenges returned for educational leaders with COVID-19 in March 2020 with an additional layer of complexity given the need and pressure for immediate solutions, which feels daunting.

How does a school district transition to an instructional delivery model that relies exclusively on remote learning in a matter of days? How do teachers decide which content gets emphasized and how to teach students through a screen? How do teachers assess learning under these unusual conditions? How does one deliver support to students with special needs? How does one determine which instructional strategies will be effective across the grade levels? Even if we have answers to these questions, how does one support the professional learning of educators so they feel confident and prepared to implement this massive shift in how education is conducted?

Families also are feeling the pressures of isolation and uncertainty. At one point in time, stay-at-home advisories were being issued like a chain of dominos across the nation, initially for two to three weeks and, ultimately, for the remainder of the school year. Nonessential employees and businesses were asked to close, and families were asked to practice "social distancing." Many did so willingly, while others failed to heed the warnings, feeling their indiscretions would be insignificant. Fortunate parents were asked to work from home, while less fortunate ones quickly signed up for unemployment or gave up on job searches after learning their children would no longer be able to attend school or daycare. Terms like "Zoom" and "Google Classroom" quickly became common educational nomenclature. Unfortunately, many families were not prepared for the transition.

Educational leaders had far more questions than answers. How does one take into account all the family circumstances happening around this issue? What about issues pertaining to equity and SES, such as determining which families have access to the internet? How do we continue to support the social and emotional needs of children during this time? Perhaps most importantly, how do we accomplish all of this while building the necessary commitment from faculty to implement the necessary changes—a faculty struggling to adapt to their own personal challenges while working from home and taking care of their own families?

A mere two months later, our world changed again following the killing caught on camera of a black man, George Floyd, in Minneapolis, Minnesota, at the hands of four white police officers. This event brought the long-standing issues of systemic racism, police brutality towards African Americans, white privilege, and hundreds of years of repression to the forefront and led to civil unrest from peaceful protests to riots and looting across the nation. Families and communities already experiencing significant distress and uncertainty due to the COVID-19 pandemic were now watching racial tensions grow and take center stage at a time when most people, neighborhoods, communities, and states were running on fumes without navigational support.

Schools remained closed during this time of rising racial tensions. The structure, routines, safety, guidance, and most importantly education that students and families depend on were only available through computer screens or cell phones. Educational leaders across the country were attempting to "pivot," another addition to the educational nomenclature in 2020, to make sure they addressed the racial tension consuming our country. It was a struggle to do so effectively via remote instruction during the final weeks of the virtual school year.

How do educational leaders address sensitive and provocative issues like systematic racism with their teachers, staff members, students, and families? How are the behaviors and actions of protestors, both peaceful and violent, processed by school-based teams and discussed by teachers and students? How are the emotions and feelings of teachers and students taken into consideration and balanced with the remaining academic expectations of the virtual school year? How should educational leaders respond to irate parents or community members who may not share the same values and beliefs during these unprecedented times? Finally, how does this get done remotely?

This is an abbreviated list of challenges linked to the unchartered territory that educational leaders face in the spring of 2020. This transformation demands that educators adapt nimbly and effectively to a wide range of new factors. While this book is not about all the steps schools need to take in order to address the COVID-19 pandemic or the racial tensions that followed, the framework and insights we illuminate will help school leaders prepare for any complex challenge that requires collaboration, creative problem solving, and attention to multiple perspectives. This book details the conditions necessary to nimbly and effectively build a strategic approach to a challenge that earns commitment from the adults who must implement the strategies designed to address the problem.

No approach to addressing significant challenges will be perfect in the first round of implementation. In order to "get it right," educators need to seek out critical feedback from stakeholders and learn from that feedback in order to create an improvement cycle that complex problems always require. Most schools are not currently set up for this kind of learning, however, and crises like the COVID-19 pandemic and the George Floyd murder have a way of spotlighting our strongest leaders while exposing the cracks in our more fractured school environments.

Responding to the pandemic and racial tension are not simply technical challenges. They are radical shifts in how we interact and learn together. Organizational and social psychology offer a wealth of resources to help educational leaders respond to these challenges. We believe our framework can assist in reshaping the learning cultures of schools, particularly with regard to how adults learn and respond to the rapidly shifting needs of their students. We are excited to share these insights with you.

Acknowledgments

I want to thank my family for being so supportive of my efforts to write this book, especially my wife, Tracey, and my four children, Brianna, JP, Gavin, and Keagan. I would also like to thank the educational leaders who have taught me, through their successes and failures, the importance of inspiration, compassion, and perseverance. I am especially grateful for the brilliant authors and educators whose contributions helped shape our framework. Lastly, I would like to thank the countless students and families who have allowed me to be a part of their school journeys; to them, I promise to keep learning and adapting in hopes of helping schools always improve.

Craig Murphy

I want to thank my colleagues at the Graduate School of Education at the University of Pennsylvania for being such helpful thought partners. I am particularly grateful to Jon Suppovitz and Michael Johanek. Much appreciation goes out to Amy Edmondson for her insightful work and research that provided a significant foundation for our own thinking. Finally, our deepest appreciation goes to the hundreds of educators and educational leaders who provided us with so much inspiration for this work.

John D'Auria

Introduction

Leadership for the future will require educational leaders to use their influence far more frequently than their positional power to enact the changes needed for durable improvement. The rapid pace of change, the deeper understanding we have acquired about human behavior, and the need for creating nimble work environments that allow for experimentation and rapid development of new ideas need an ecosystem where people feel safe to learn and are motivated by inspiration to achieve exceptional results in teaching and learning. Inspired people gain energy and fortitude to overcome the inertia and fears that hold them back. The status quo, while comfortable, will not help us close the achievement, resources, language, and special needs gaps that exist in schools today.

James Baldwin wrote, "Not everything that is faced can be changed, but nothing can be changed that is not faced" (1962). Influential school leaders inspire educators to face the myriad of challenges confronting schools and commit to strategies aimed at improvement. People are not motivated to change their behavior simply by acquiring new knowledge. Acquired knowledge must be integrated into their emotional senses in order to make transformational change. This dynamic played out in South Carolina where for years government officials and citizens heard and read about the symbolic and negative impact that flying a Confederate flag had on their citizens, particularly African Americans. Despite that knowledge, nothing changed until 21-year-old, white supremacist Dylann Roof killed nine African Americans attending a Bible Study group at the well-known Emanuel African Methodist Episcopal Church. Amazingly, instead of reacting with violence, the surviving members of the church, their families, and concerned citizens responded peacefully and with forgiveness. People were moved, which ultimately led South Carolina leaders to remove the Confederate flag from display on the grounds of South Carolina's State House. Interestingly, this issue recently resurfaced when NASCAR made the decision to ban the Confederate flag from all races following the Black Lives Matter movement, which was reinvigorated following the murder of George Floyd. Despite a public outpouring of support and praise for NASCAR, vitriolic attacks followed. A noose was discovered in the garage of NASCAR's only African American driver, Bubba Wallace. While the FBI ultimately determined the noose was placed prior to Wallace's use of the garage, it was inspiring to witness other drivers tacitly declare racism does not have a home in NASCAR by pushing Wallace's car to the front row before a race at Talladega Superspeedway in Alabama.

Simply put, inspiration occurs when knowledge is integrated with emotions. We advocate for an approach that taps into this powerful dynamic. Following our recommendations does not necessarily guarantee success; however, doing so raises the probability that issues will be addressed deeply, with a commitment to gain needed improvements.

Foundations of the Framework

The fields of social and organizational psychology have made significant contributions to numerous industries including marketing, finance, sales, healthcare, and social services. Our framework for educational leaders integrates numerous principles from social and organizational psychology and adapts numerous models from renowned authors from both fields to make them specifically applicable to education. Our readings and experiences have taught us there is no shortage of great minds within psychology.

Cialdini (2006), for example, discussed "weapons of influence" and how they are used relentlessly in marketing, sales, and advertising. Gladwell (2005) introduced the world to "The Power of Thinking Without Thinking" in his best-selling book *Blink*. His book was later expanded by Daniel Kahneman (2011), who helped us understand the juxtaposition of thinking both fast and slow. Bronson and Merryman (2011) proposed a new way of thinking about children by focusing on external events and societal changes rather than personal characteristics. Recently, renowned social psychologists Thomas Gilovich and Lee Ross discussed how individuals can benefit from insights from social psychology research in their book, *The Wisest One in the Room* (2015).

Similarly, Oshry (2007) discussed the importance of seeing the system and the consequences of system blindness in his book *Seeing Systems: Unlocking the Mysteries of Organizational Life*. Brene Brown spotlighted the importance of belonging in a society that has become increasingly isolated and disconnected and emphasized a direct correlation between true belonging and self-acceptance. Edmondson (2019) helped define *Psychological Safety* and its importance in helping organizations thrive. Writing about consequences for organizations without sufficient psychological safety, Edmonson wrote:

> Knowledgeable, skilled, well-meaning people cannot always contribute what they know at that critical moment on the job when it is needed. Sometimes this is because they fail to recognize the need for their knowledge. More often, it's because they're reluctant to stand out, be wrong, or offend the boss. For knowledge work to flourish, the workplace must be one where people feel able to share their knowledge! (Kindle Locations, pp. 333–334).

Finally, Charles Duhigg (2016) redefined the term efficiency in his book *Smarter, Faster, Better: The Secrets of Being Productive in Life and Business* and specifically explored concepts like internal and external locus of control and its impact on motivation in children.

Given the substantial empirical support that is considered the trademark of social psychology research, as well as the rich contributions that experts in the field of organizational psychology have made to businesses and institutions throughout the world, we believe it is critical for educators to integrate lessons learned from both social and organizational psychology into their practices now more than ever.

Schools and educators face an ever-growing set of complex challenges that require knowledge, skills, collaboration, creativity, resources, and effective leadership to address. No matter the challenge, making progress will require commitment and deep engagement from everyone. Those qualities cannot be delivered, however, by commands and regulations. In order to raise the probability of success, district, building, and classroom leaders will need to influence their constituents to engage in and authentically embrace recommended strategies and approaches. Maximizing our influence is a central tenet of this book.

Aronson, Wilson, and Akert (2010) define *social influence* as "the influences that people have upon the beliefs, feelings, and behavior of others" (p. 3). The implications of this are staggering. It is essential for school leaders, classroom teachers, specialists, students, and families to understand social influence and the role it plays in today's schools. School leaders are challenged often to create change within their districts and/or buildings. Influencing people to change is not easy, particularly if the changes you want to see are ones that require people to own the change and not simply comply with a directive. How do school leaders influence educators to make changes in their instruction or interaction styles with students, parents, and colleagues?

Teachers are greeted each morning by a classroom of diverse learners with different educational and family backgrounds. They are expected to move their "group" of students through a prescribed curriculum that often includes standardized tests designed to measure student progress—though in practice, test results are used often to document teacher and district failures and/or accomplishments. How can teachers challenge students from diverse backgrounds, establish learning climates that are both unconditionally supportive and welcoming, and simultaneously engage families and parents in their child's education?

Specialists such as occupational therapists, speech and language therapists, learning center teachers, math coaches, physical education teachers, art teachers, and music teachers also play critical roles in the education of children. Yet who determines what that role is? How can we optimize the skills and knowledge of these specialists so struggling children can receive maximum benefits and enjoy their time at school?

Students enter classrooms with dramatically different perceptions about the role that school plays in their lives. Some feel education is critical for their future goals, such as becoming a lawyer or doctor like their parents. Others see school as an inconvenience or temporary holding place until their inevitable drop-out in high school. Countless perceptions fall along the continuum of perceiving education as a bridge to success or a persistent reminder of accumulating frustrations and failures. From where do these perceptions come? How can we change them?

Without exception, families play an integral role in the education of their children. Some "choose" to be involved and supportive, either because they believe in the importance of education or simply because they enjoy privileges that allow them to do so. Other families take a less active role because they (a) may not have experienced the benefit of education firsthand, (b) are not comfortable and/or equipped to join conversations that do not appear to include them, (c) are unable to juggle the countless responsibilities they face in order to become actively involved, and/or (d) their cultural influences frame the role of parents differently. How can we help **ALL** families understand the importance of education and find their seat at the table to support their children's efforts in school?

It is not the goal of this book to answer these challenging questions. Rather, drawing from social and organizational psychology research, we focus on creating conditions and skill sets that allow educators and their constituents to engage in a process that provides them a deeper understanding of the problems they face. Such collaboratively-built understanding, coupled with a culture that provides sufficient psychological safety, makes it possible to develop and embrace strategies and approaches that have a reasonable-to-high chance of achieving improvement and gaining essential insights. Nothing is a sure bet in education, but we believe the framework we offer will raise the probability of success.

Regardless of the specific changes needed to improve schools, nimble learning will be at the core of how a school or district moves from where they are now to new and improved ways of supporting the needs of their students. Rapid changes in technology, brain research, our understanding of disabilities, the impact of trauma on learning, and the social-emotional connection to cognition are just a small sample of significant shifts that have the potential to impact teaching, learning, and educational practices. Many schools, however, are not set up to access and learn from these new discoveries. In the absence of sustained improvement, schools often continue to prepare their students the way they have been doing so for decades. In some contexts, schools with solid reputations based on standardized test scores and college acceptances lack a sense of urgency to change.

Where a sense of urgency is apparent, often there are numerous fires to extinguish and pressing issues demanding attention above and beyond normal teaching and learning routines. In either context, lack of strategic interventions limits opportunities for effectively preparing students for rapidly-changing economic and global challenges. Simultaneously, many schools are experiencing a shift in demographics that require a better understanding of culture, language, and experiences that are often different from the student populations of the past (Mordechay & Orfield, 2017).

What unites schools across multiple domains is the critical need for educators to become facile with new educational findings, learn new approaches, and understand more deeply how a student's context influences his or her learning. Given the pace of change, the sense that many faculty feel overwhelmed, and the lack of urgency that is often a hallmark of schools with previously established good reputations, we need a new approach that focuses on *nimble learning*. Nimble learning means gaining comfort with mistakes, errors, and failure so learning can be turned into insights and improvements. Nimble learning not only benefits educators; it helps students prepare for their ever-changing futures.

Because change is complex, educational leadership must extend beyond principals or a few administrators. When leadership is distributed, change can be managed more effectively. Involved faculty who understand the issues limiting progress will be more committed to approaches aimed at strengthening improvement (Block, 2011). Because time is short and schools still rely primarily on principals to lead the charge, solutions to knotty problems often are dictated to staff prior to establishing a deeper understanding of underlying issues and securing a commitment of stakeholders to embrace the needed changes. The lack of sufficient progress in closing achievement gaps and making progress on important issues is linked to treating the symptoms of problems rather than their root causes. By tapping into insights from both social and organizational psychology, we recommend a new set of lenses to both examine and analyze problems, as well as an "engagement of stakeholders" approach that will increase the probability that root causes of problems will be addressed successfully. This combination leads to more vibrant and inclusive school communities.

Challenge of Educational Leadership

Although our framework offers educational leaders an alternative approach to understanding and solving complex problems in schools, a common barrier stands in the way. Specifically, educational leaders must reflect on how they spend their time "at work." Supovitz, D'Auria, and Spillane (2019) discuss four major areas that typically absorb the time and efforts of educational leaders. The authors originally named three areas and later incorporated personal well-being. The four areas include maintenance, putting out fires, strategic improvement, and personal well-being. Ideally, educational leaders would distribute their time evenly across these four areas.

Maintenance involves the innumerable daily tasks that comprise the work of schools. For example, educational leaders are often tasked with preparing reports, providing feedback, organizing meetings, designing schedules, balancing budgets, running safety drills, and organizing parent committees. These tasks must be completed on a regular basis, and educational leaders are ultimately responsible for making sure they are done correctly.

Putting Out Fires involves the unpredictable but inevitable challenges in schools that emerge and must be addressed in a timely fashion. An educational leader may have to address an angry parent who unexpectedly shows up in the main office, a leak in the cafeteria that disrupts the lunch period, or a bomb scare that involves police and local officials. These events are not scheduled but demand the attention of school leaders and take immediate precedent.

Strategic Improvement Efforts involve long-term planning efforts designed to address systemic problems and implement durable solutions. Educational leaders might develop long-term plans to close achievement gaps, convene a group of teachers and staff members to produce more operational efficiencies, spend time reviewing and strengthening curricular offerings, and explore options for increasing faculty capacity. Although these activities are critical for school improvement, especially during a time of rapidly-changing advancements in technology and instruction, they are rarely prioritized and often get bumped off the radar of educational leaders due to demands related to maintenance and putting out fires.

Personal Well-Being is often considered a luxury for educational leaders. Often referred to as self-care, educational leaders need to identify and prioritize sources of energy they can access to sustain the demanding pace of their work in schools.

Job performance of educational leaders is impacted negatively when they are over-stressed and on the verge of burnout. Staff meetings become inefficient or less engaging; teacher evaluations lack insight and value; community engagement and rewarding time with students disappear; their overall health declines. Unfortunately, as with leaders from other industries, personal well-being is neglected often by educational leaders. The COVID-19 pandemic certainly has altered the balance for many educational leaders.

These four categories often intersect. As putting out fires takes up more time, it leaves less time for maintenance and improvement, which may increase the probability of more fires emerging. If strategic planning consumes too much time, maintenance of regular operations suffers. Looking at general patterns, we find that putting out fires and maintaining the day-to-day operations of schools account for the greatest percentage of educator workdays, leaving little time for strategic improvement efforts and personal well-being. The Distribution of Effort for educational leaders feeling overwhelmed by putting out fires and maintenance leaves little room for strategic improvement and personal well-being.

We fully recognize that even under the best of circumstances, time will not be equally distributed across each of the four domains, nor will any pattern remain constant. All four, however, are essential. Strategic planning allows educators time to discuss and work on solutions to long-standing issues and better serve students. When this important work gets short shrift, the expertise and insights of educators are lost. A lack of focus on strategic planning often leads to a superficial understanding of complex problems which, in turn, dramatically lowers the probability that interventions or improvement strategies will work. Exhausted principals who spend most of their time "maintaining" and "putting out fires" have little energy to focus on making educational improvements. Setting aside time to do so can feel like a singular, lonely pursuit because they are not invested in a more collaborative process that allows for greater understanding underlying problems. Rushing strategic improvement efforts leads to misunderstanding problems and superficial compliance with recommended strategies from educational leaders.

The typical distribution of time noted above left many educational leaders and schools in a weakened position to manage the crisis caused by the COVID-19 pandemic in the spring of 2020. When schools closed and educators began to work remotely, the time balance shifted. Out of necessity, more time and a much higher premium was placed on strategic planning as educational leaders sought to support teachers and serve students and families under extraordinarily difficult conditions. Many leadership teams were not practiced in the kind of planning and creative problem-solving needed to address the challenges created by this pandemic. Many were forced to use weakened "strategic collaborative planning" muscles rather than more practiced "putting out fires" and "maintenance" ones.

Framework

The framework we recommend in this book will allow educational leaders to become nimble at learning and more effective at working collaboratively to remove obstacles that block the improvements and changes needed to craft schools that better meet the present and future needs of students. Our framework involves a set of strategies and lenses aimed at improving our vision and maximizing our influence so educators and leaders can unlock their creativity, develop needed improvements, and create new approaches to problem solving. At the same time, this framework provides a model for the kind of thinking and collaboration that benefits the students served as they prepare for a rapidly-changing future. Effective leadership that maximizes group potential addresses a number of underlying issues that create fires which, in turn, consume a significant amount of educational leaders' time. The collaborative process we recommend builds commitment to the improvement strategies along the way.

Our framework emphasizes seeing the system as a four-by-three model. Part I of the book, Improving Your Vision, explains our framework in two chapters. Chapter 1, Four Distinct Perspectives, reviews the four levels that are commonly found in schools. Consistent with Oshry's work, the four levels include the superintendent (Tops), principal (Middles), classroom teachers and specialists (Bottoms), and students and their families (Customers). The interdependent nature of schools is discussed, as well as the importance of looking at problems from each of the four distinct vantage points. Chapter 2, Seeing the System in 3D, reviews the three dimensions of our model. Specifically, the dimensions are what we should be considering when attempting to understand problems and generate solutions that will be implemented with fidelity. They include the surface-level dimension (i.e., behaviors and actions), the below-the-surface dimension (i.e., feelings and emotions), and the systems-dimension (i.e., values and beliefs). The chapter includes a discussion of the implications of focusing too much, or neglecting to consider, one of the dimensions in our work as educational leaders.

Conditions for Change

Part II, Conditions for Change, includes four chapters that focus on aspects of educational leadership we consider to be vital, each of which is informed by numerous principles from both social and organizational psychology. Chapter 3, Balancing Psychological Safety with Accountability, discusses why this balance is so important for educational leaders and the consequences for schools and school districts when they fail to achieve it. We will examine how educational leaders prioritize psychological safety and accountability. Finally, we discuss strategies for assessing psychological safety and implications of accountability for educator evaluations.

Part II, Chapter 4, Strengthening Belonging, explores the different definitions of belonging and the theoretical underpinnings that are thought to either fortify or dilute those feelings. These include concepts such as group cohesiveness, social norms, core values, and school mission statements. In addition, strategies for increasing belonging are discussed, as well as common indicators for school environments considered to have a strong sense of belonging amongst their staff members. Lastly, the consequences for schools, students, and families when a strong sense of belonging is absent are examined.

Part II, Chapter 5, Engaging in Open and Honest Communication, discusses the importance of establishing the necessary conditions and habits that allow open and honest communication to exist within a school environment. The concept of nondiscussables is examined, as well as the relationship between the number of nondiscussables and the communication patterns present within a school. Other topics in the chapter include the role of power differentials in establishing strong communication habits and how to manage disagreements in a way that is both respectful and productive. Finally, strategies for creating the conditions for open and honest communication are specified.

Part II, Chapter 6, Encouraging Experimentation, examines the importance of nimble learning within educational settings. Since some schools and educators often try to avoid making mistakes and taking chances, valuable opportunities for learning are often missed. The chapter includes important discussions related to mindset, resiliency, and other concepts from the rapidly expanding field that addresses social and emotional learning. Finally, the chapter spotlights how leaders approach times of uncertainty and crisis, and how these times often expose fractured leadership teams because of their inability to tolerate experimentation and failures.

Included in each of the chapters from Parts I and II of the book are critical terms and concepts we have learned from social and organizational psychology. In some instances, landmark studies (e.g., Asch Line Study) are briefly discussed to provide appropriate context to better understand how these ideas helped shape our framework. We thought it was important to define the terminology we used throughout the book and to provide specific examples of how these concepts manifest in educational environments.

Applying the Framework

Part III of the book focuses on the application of the framework within educational settings and includes two chapters. Chapter 7, A Leadership Guide—Moving from Theory to Practice, is a step by step outline for integrating the framework into existing educational settings. Chapter 8, Preparing for Change, includes strategies for (a) identifying current practices that might be incompatible with the framework, (b) developing the conditions necessary for change, and (c) troubleshooting likely challenges that school-based teams might face when attempting to introduce the framework to their system. The final two chapters provide comprehensive case studies, one from an elementary school and one from a high school, where teams are applying the framework to a specific problem they are trying to solve. In the elementary example, the implementation of the framework is explicitly structured with concrete identifiers that allow the reader to follow the sequence of the framework from start-to-finish. In the high school example, the framework is more embedded in the exchanges you read about within the context of the vignette. We hope these varied approaches help to deepen your understanding of the framework and give you the confidence to dive in and use it within your own context.

We have also included numerous vignettes throughout the chapters that reflect our experiences working in schools and consulting to school-based teams and leaders. To protect the confidentiality of our colleagues and our consultation clients, all characters in the vignettes have been given pseudonyms and sensitive details have been adapted, which provides anonymity without altering the lessons learned from the stories. In some cases, multiple stories or experiences have been integrated into one example.

References

Aronson, E., Wilson, T. D., & Akert, R. M. (2010). *Social psychology* (7th ed.). Pearson.

Baldwin, J. (January 14, 1962). *As much truth as one can bear.* The New York Times, Section T, 11.

Block, P. (2011). *Flawless consulting: A guide to getting your expertise used* (3rd ed.). Pfeiffer.

Bronson, P., & Merryman, A. (2011). *NurtureShock: New thinking about children* (Reprint ed.). Twelve.

Cialdini, R. B. (2006). *Influence: The psychology of persuasion* (Revised. ed.). Harper Business.

Duhigg, C. (2016). *Smarter, faster, better: The secrets of being productive in life and business.* Random House.

Edmondson, A. C. (2019). *The fearless organization: Creating psychological safety in the workplace for learning, innovation, and growth.* Wiley and Sons.

Edmondson, A. C., Roberto, M. R., Bohmer, R. M. J., Ferlins, E. M., & Feldman, L. R. (2005). The recovery window: Organizational learning following ambiguous threats. In M. Farjoun & W. Starbuc (Eds.), *Organization at the limits: NASA and the Columbia disaster* (pp. 220–245). Retrieved from https://doi.org/10.1080/02626667.2018.1560449.

Gilovich, T., & Ross, L. (2015). *The wisest one in the room: How you can benefit from social psychology's most powerful insights.* Free Press.

Gladwell, M. (2005). *Blink: The power of thinking without thinking* (1st ed.). Little, Brown and Company.

Kahneman, D. (2011). *Thinking, fast and slow.* Farrar, Straus and Giroux.

Mordechay, K., & Orfield, G. (2017). Demographic transformation in a policy vacuum: The changing face of U.S. metropolitan society and challenges for public schools. *The Educational Forum, 81*(2), 193–203. Retrieved from https://doi.org/10.1080/00131725.2017.1280758.

Oshry, B. (2007). *Seeing systems: Unlocking the mysteries of organizational life* (2nd ed.). Berrett-Koehler Publishers.

Supovitz, J., D'Auria, J., & Spillane, J. (2019). *Meaningful & sustainable school improvement with distributed leadership.* CPRE Research Reports. Retrieved from https://repository.upenn.edu/cpre_researchreports/112.

PART I

Improving Your Vision

1

Four Distinct Perspectives

Introduction

Letters were mailed out to over 100 teachers informing them that their contracts would not be renewed for the next school year. Phone calls quickly flooded the superintendent's office. Building principals held private meetings with teachers and parents. Teachers struggled to discern if they should look for new jobs or wait patiently, hoping to be rehired if the proposed school budget was approved. In the community, a parent group created a Facebook page titled "Save our Schools." Hundreds of signatures were collected and plans were made to attend the next school committee meeting in force. The parent group advocated that funds be diverted from the police and fire department to the schools in order to rehire the teachers. Younger students remained blissfully unaware of the rising tensions, while older students questioned the quality and value of their education and wondered aloud what their school would look like with fewer teachers. The decision by school districts to implement a reduction-in-force (RIF) process typically has a ripple effect throughout the school and family communities. Examining the different perspectives of key stakeholders in reduction-in-force situations illuminates the importance of the first component of our framework.

The school superintendent ultimately is responsible for balancing the school budget and presenting it to the school committee and town officials for formal approval. When financial complications make it difficult to accomplish that goal in a timely manner, budget cuts are proposed. In most cases, teacher salaries represent the largest percentage of school budgets. Superintendents often initiate a reduction-in-force, even though they feel confident a majority of teachers who receive nonrenewal notices will be "rehired" once the school budget is formally approved. Superintendents understand and appreciate the difference between proposed cuts and anticipated actual cuts for the following school year, as they ultimately are responsible for proposing reductions-in-force. Given the level of inherent uncertainty when working with school committees and town officials, superintendents often are unable to share their anticipated expectations or hopes related to staffing until a final school budget is approved. Superintendents often sit alone with enormous stress and responsibility on their shoulders during challenging times.

Building principals view situations from a different perspective than superintendents. They participate in district-wide leadership meetings and, therefore, have an overall understanding of the challenges facing school districts. They also work directly with teachers and specialists and interact with students and families daily. In addition, building principals often serve as conduits between their school community and the school district's administrative team. The strength of this connection often determines whether school districts are cohesive or divided. Principals balance the needs and wants of their school communities with the resources and capabilities of school districts. Principals are constantly challenged to understand and respond to the needs of their students, families, and teachers, while simultaneously considering and implementing directives from administration. When these forces are aligned, principals likely find their jobs rewarding and manageable. When they conflict, which is often the case when a reduction-in-force is implemented, principals struggle to manage uncomfortable and stressful situations.

The perspective of classroom teachers can be compared to "frontline" workers. Classroom teachers, specialists (e.g., physical education teachers, art teachers, music teachers, special education teachers, school psychologists, occupational therapists, speech and language therapists), and paraprofessionals work directly with students on a daily basis and regularly interact with families. For the purpose of this chapter, we use the term "teachers" to refer to all frontline educators.

Teachers are tasked with educating students. The success of those students, often measured by standardized test scores, is considered an indicator of whether or not teachers have been successful. Teachers typically are involved in discussions and meetings at the building-level; participation at the administrative-level is minimal. The perspective of teachers is influenced by direct accountability for student achievement and limited control for how schools operate at the district-level. Thus, when reductions-in-force are initiated, teachers often feel the impact most directly, as they are most at risk for losing their jobs. Given their lack of input when decisions are made at the district-level to make budget cuts, it is understandable that teachers often feel powerless and disenfranchised when their positions are eliminated, even if they are likely to be reinstated.

The perspective of students and families can be compared to that of a consumer. If education and opportunities for socialization are the products being sold by school districts, students and families are the ones purchasing those products and providing feedback regarding levels of satisfaction. Although the collective voice of parents and families is typically louder than that of students, students are more vocal consumers, particularly at the secondary level. When reductions-in-force occur, parents and students often react instantly, expressing their discontent publicly believing the product delivered by school districts is diluted and undervalued. Parents and families have direct contact and strong relationships with teachers to whom they feel personally connected and indebted because of care and support given to their children. Therefore, when news breaks that teachers are losing their jobs, parents and students show up in force.

School districts as systems are not unique. Organizational psychologists have examined the various perspectives of their stakeholders and found significant implications for educational leaders. Most notably, Barry Oshry and Roger Schwarz significantly influenced the development of our framework. We acknowledge these authors have significantly impacted our thinking and idea formation.

Understanding the (School) System

Oshry (2007) suggests four distinct perspectives that are almost always present and impacting an issue. These perspectives represent views from:

- ◆ **Tops or Senior Management**—Often represented by members of the C-Suite. Within a school district, they would be superintendents and other district-wide leaders.
- ◆ **Middles of Middle Management**—Those who lead programs or divisions. Within a school district, principals and K-12 directors would be examples.
- ◆ **Bottoms or Line Workers**—These people provide direct services to customers and clients. In a school setting, they would be teachers.
- ◆ **Customers or Clients**—These are the consumers of product. In education, they include students, parents, and members of the community.

Educational leaders must understand that, in order to fully grasp an issue or problem, one must look at it from each of the above perspectives and vantage points to make informed decisions. According to Oshry, problems occur when one experiences "spatial blindness." He writes,

> Generally, if we are paying attention, we know what life is like for us in our part of the system. Other parts of the system are, for the most part, invisible to us. We do not know what others are experiencing, what their worlds are like, what issues they are dealing with, what

dilemmas they are facing, what stresses they are under-going. To make matters worse, sometimes we think we know when in fact we do not. We have our beliefs, myths, and prejudices, which we accept as the truth and which become the bases of our actions. This blindness to other parts of the system—which we call spatial blindness—is a source of considerable misunder-standing, conflict, and diminished system contribution.

Oshry suggests that each of these *perspectives* provides a potent and illuminating set of data. In education, superintendents *see* a wide range of issues and develop a sense of deep accountability for the successes and failures of the system. Principals are torn—pulled between the needs of teachers and families, yet accountable to the administrative team. While they hold power, they often must request permission to act. This leaves many feeling inadequate. Teachers feel vulnerable because they are affected by things over which they have no control. Lastly, the perspective of families and students often leads them feeling neglected. "They are not getting the attention they feel they deserve; they are shunted from one person to another; products and services are not coming to them as fast as they want, at the level of quality they want, and at a satisfactory price (p. 1)."

Each perspective is important. It is imperative to have a clear sense of how each perspective informs a particular issue in order to resolve the matter or make improvements. Failure to do so limits our *vision*. Understanding the perspectives of others is key to how we maximize our influence as leaders.

When we experience "spatial blindness," the quality of collaboration is diminished, and people move from critiquing ideas and strategies toward personal attacks, gossip, and com-plaining. Interestingly, significant organizational improvements can begin simply by crafting ways for people to share their perspectives and experiences with others. While this is not complicated, it sometimes is easier said than done. Workers and leaders frequently operate from the erroneous idea that ev-eryone has access to the same information and experiences the organization similarly. Further, it is challenging for employees with less authority and power to share their perspectives with those above them for fear their experiences will be seen as critical of leadership.

Finding ways to share perspectives and experiences is challenging. Recognizing that there are varied "realities" within an organization is an initial and vital step. Ascertaining how each role experiences the organizations is a solid second step. Understanding the complexities, challenges, and feelings of those from different vantage points ensures one is well-equipped with vital data and information that will inform critical decisions and recommendations for improvement.

We regularly hear stories from educators about their supportive and understanding supervisors. Ironically, these stories often are followed immediately with stories about how their bosses "don't get it." A group of principals, for example, once shared about feeling torn between the amount of responsibility they feel for their schools and the accountability they expect for work done by their teachers—describing it as akin to riding a gerbil wheel. When asked by the administrative team to think strategically about ways to bring achievement at their schools to new heights, the group of principals expressed concerns about their ability to do so because of how much time is spent putting out fires or filling in for absent staff. When they describe these challenges to the administrative team, they receive a modicum of empathy and acknowledgment. They also share stories about receiving emails and urgent messages requiring an immediate response when they are home sick or caring for an ailing child. "They just don't get it" is a recurring refrain.

If members of the administrative team could magically be "principals for a day," they would experience viscerally the complex issues and dilemmas principals face. These same principals are reluctant to resist requests for new initiatives or additional work fearing they will be viewed as unenthusiastic, negative employees. This blocked channel of communication prevents a superintendent from truly *seeing* experiences from the perspective of principals, whose reluctance to share their experiences in an honest and authentic way compounds the problem of spatial blindness.

Exiting the Gerbil Wheel

When consulting schools experiencing spatial blindness, we often gather together two groups representing different vantage points. Recently, we brought together principals with central office staff. Principals were asked to discuss with each other their response to the following question:

> What do you want your colleagues who are district leaders to better understand about your work and the challenges you face that you think they don't see or understand?

After some discussion amongst themselves, principals shared their collective thinking with the district leaders sitting across from them. District leaders were asked to listen "in stereo" to what the principals shared—meaning not only the content of their thoughts but their feelings as well. The central office team then was asked to summarize what had been shared. In turn, principals stated whether or not the district team correctly captured their ideas and feelings. If they did not, the principals shared what was missing, and the central office team made a second attempt to capture the perspective of the principals correctly.

The principals shared how challenging it is to leave their buildings for extended periods during the week to attend meetings at the central office. They also shared that these meetings regularly went well beyond scheduled end times, which left important matters unattended in their own buildings. They said a large percentage of information communicated at these meetings could be sent via email. When the district leaders attempted to summarize the perspective of the principals, they immediately started to "solve the problem," as well as refute some of what the principals shared. While discussion and disagreement can be a part of this exercise, the critical initial goal is to foster understanding.

We then asked the district leaders a parallel question, and principals attempted to summarize, in stereo, what they heard. The central office team then shared whether or not principals captured the essence of what was expressed. Central office administrators discussed how they often are relied on to "bail out" principals when initiatives they launch go awry. They expressed how it would be helpful if they were involved in an initiative before it launched so their insights could be part of the planning. This simple exchange shifted the understanding of both parties and expanded their views of how others experience the organization. A shift in understanding provides a deeper appreciation for the experiences of others, as well as a more profound understanding of why communication gets distorted. These shifts minimize blame. While new understanding can be helpful, it does not lead to sustained improvement without dialogue and creative problem solving, which we will discuss more directly when examining the four critical conditions necessary to support sustained improvement.

Social Psychology and the Four Perspectives

To advance our understanding of the importance of the four perspectives, we turn to social psychology and, specifically, to the role of social cognition. Aronson and Aronson (2018) defined social cognition as "the study of how people come to believe what they do; how they explain, remember, predict, make decisions, and evaluate themselves and others; and why these processes so frequently produce errors" (p. 14). Clearly, the role of social cognition is extremely powerful when considering how the four perspectives develop, impact decision-making, and inform how the different stakeholders evaluate themselves and each other.

A primary contribution of research on social cognition is the creation of mental categories or groups, often referred to as schemas, that help us organize information. Schemas can be extremely valuable and efficient, like when we learn to avoid dark alleys at night because they might be unsafe. They also can be problematic when our generalizations lead to stereotypes and prejudice. In these cases, social categorizations lead to the formation of different groups, which ultimately creates an "Us vs. Them" mentality (Aronson, Wilson, & Akert, 2010). This is relevant to the first part of our framework for educational leaders, as the four perspectives represent four distinct groups of people based on certain characteristics. Depending on one's membership, an in-group bias is likely to emerge.

A teacher, for example, may develop an in-group bias that says teachers are the most important subgroup of educators because they are directly responsible for teaching children. They instantly empathize with colleagues, as they know exactly what it takes to run a classroom and keep students progressing for a 180-day school year. Unfortunately, social categorization can also result in the perception of out-group homogeneity, meaning members of the in-group perceive that members of the out-group are all alike. For educators, this might result in teachers developing negative perceptions of superintendents. Groups of teachers may join conversations about the luxuries of administrators making comments like, "I wish I had time for lunch" or "I don't even have time to go to the bathroom during the day." Similar conversations likely occur within the other stakeholder groups based on their intimate knowledge and understanding of their daily challenges and demands, and their lack of insight regarding the other groups. Ultimately, the in-group bias fosters hostility and resentment resulting in poor communication, a fractured sense of belonging, and a weakened commitment to the mission of schools. Given what social psychologists have learned about the in-group bias and the perception of out-group homogeneity, educational leaders must bring these groups together to actively cultivate a shared understanding of the challenges facing schools.

A second relevant concept from the social cognition literature is confirmation bias. Confirmation bias refers to the process of seeking out information that confirms our current beliefs while ignoring, or even rejecting, information that refutes our current beliefs. During reductions-in-force, for example, teachers might immediately point to the decision of eliminating teacher positions as yet another example that administrators do not value teachers and, instead, place a greater priority on administrative positions. When it is pointed out to them that administrator positions were also eliminated, teachers might dismiss the additional information by saying something like, "Yeah, but only three administrator positions were eliminated, and over fifty teaching positions were eliminated." Although the proportion of administrator lay-offs may indicate equity, teachers might fail to consider this because it does not align with their view of administration. They have developed specific beliefs about administrators, and behaviors that align with those beliefs are instantly recognized to strengthen those beliefs. When administrators behave in ways that are inconsistent with teacher beliefs, those behaviors are considered outliers and quickly dismissed. Knowing the power of confirmation bias, individuals from each of the four perspectives should be encouraged to actively seek out information about members from other groups to counteract their preconceived notions.

The importance of truly understanding the four perspectives for educational leaders cannot be overstated. Sharing that collective understanding with involved stakeholder groups can often be the difference between successful and unsuccessful initiatives within schools. In the reduction-in-force example, by helping others understand the implications of an unbalanced budget the superintendent has the potential to bring different stakeholder groups together to effect change in support of the schools and students. Actively seeking out and examining the four perspectives is the first lens we recommend for educators committed to sustainable change and improving their schools. Equally important is the second lens, the Three Dimensions, which we describe in the next chapter.

References

Aronson, E., & Aronson, J. (2018). *The social animal* (12th ed.). Worth Publishers.

Aronson, E., Wilson, T. D., & Akert, R. M. (2010). *Social psychology* (7th ed.). Pearson.

Oshry, B. (2007). *Seeing systems: Unlocking the mysteries of organizational life* (2nd ed.). Berrett-Koehler Publishers.

2

Seeing the System in 3D

In addition to the four vantage points that allow educational leaders to better understand situations they are confronted with on a daily basis, each problem consists of three dimensions that must be considered prior to taking action. Each problem includes a surface-level dimension (behaviors and actions), below-the-surface dimension (feelings and attitudes), and system dimension (beliefs and values). Educational leaders must consider what is being communicated at each dimension, either directly or indirectly, and how those considerations can be used to improve their understanding of a problem. The ability to see in 3D enables educational leaders to be highly effective in assessing challenging situations and harnessing their influence for the purpose of implementing durable solutions.

Surface-Level Dimension

Observable behavior or action typically represents the starting point for most problems in education. Whether a school administrator is concerned about the number of students who have been placed out-of-district, a principal is concerned that teachers are not arriving to school in accordance with their contract and allowing sufficient time to prepare for the school day, or a classroom teacher is concerned about a student who never has a healthy lunch or snack, the surface-level dimension encompasses problems that exist on the surface, grab our immediate attention, and demand a response. Regarding the increasing number of out-of-district placements, school-based teams may be encouraged to offer assistant supports for challenging students. For tardy teachers, an attendance monitoring system requiring they sign in and out each morning and afternoon may be implemented. For the student with insufficient nutrition, a snack bin filled with an assortment of healthy snacks may be provided by the student's teacher. Issues at the surface level are easily identified, and logical solutions can be applied quickly and directly.

The value of interventions targeting problems manifested at the surface-level dimension is they have potential to produce immediate, visible, and concrete results. A teacher's new snack bin ensures a hungry student has a healthy snack to eat each day. These solutions send a message to the target audience that the problem is unacceptable, that action is being taken promptly and decisively, and that those who expressed concerns were heard and are being supported. Such interventions, however, may not address the root cause of the presenting problems. Solutions, therefore, might only address symptoms of a larger problem. Consider the following example:

Dr. Beverly Tatum's national bestseller *Why Are All the Black Kids Sitting Together in the Cafeteria* (2017) illustrates what starts out to be a surface-level problem, although the book focuses on far more than the topography of the problem. In high school cafeterias across America, students often sit in segregated groups, leading concerned educators to question why their student population remains segregated at times. In a recent consultation case, it was shared with us that some staff and students in one high school in the Northeast refers to a section of their cafeteria as "Cafrica." The administrative team at the high school was horrified by the term and ashamed when they discovered that it had been used so casually and for so many years. The surface-level dimension of this problem is evident to students, teachers, and administrators. Students continue to sit in groups that are, to some degree, determined by race. Educators who seek to "solve" the problem by focusing on the surface-level dimension, develop solutions that target behaviors and actions. Numerous options would directly address the symptoms of the problem. A high school might implement assigned seating during lunch, for example. Or, perhaps integrated classrooms could sit in assigned areas to avoid segregated lunch tables. These solutions would immediately address the surface-level problems, but the underlying causes for the segregation and potential strategies to create a more inclusive school would remain untouched. So, when exactly should educational leaders consider the surface-level dimension?

The surface-level dimension consists of two primary groups of concerns: behaviors and actions. Educators viewing problems at the surface-level are focused on the "what" rather than the "why." For example, educational leaders are often faced with the challenge of teachers arriving late for work, showing up late for meetings, or missing important deadlines (e.g., submitting final grades or progress reports). Some might argue the "why" in these situations is not important, as the problem behaviors are simply unacceptable and must change. Therefore, solutions often are behaviorally-oriented, meaning they incorporate principles of reinforcement and punishment and focus on observable behaviors to determine if change has occurred.

The surface-level dimension is fueled by Fundamental Attribution Error (FAE), a key concept from social psychology literature. Aronson and Aronson (2018) state, "The term fundamental attribution error refers to a human tendency to overestimate the importance of personality or dispositional factors relative to situational or environmental influences when describing and explaining why people do what they do" (p. 38). The FAE identifies a problem by noticing the behaviors and/or actions of others, and then attributing those behaviors and actions to personality or dispositional factors. Teachers who show up minutes before school each morning and appear unprepared for the start of the day are deemed lazy, lacking in commitment to their classroom and students, and unmotivated to put in the time it takes to be a great teacher. Ironically, research on attribution theory suggests the human tendency is to consider situational and environmental factors when describing and explaining our own behavior. Principals may be quick to criticize teachers who barely beat the bell each morning but be far less critical of themselves when regularly arriving late to school after attending meetings with other principals and administrators. In this scenario, principals are well-aware of the environmental and situational influences that impact their arrival time and are unlikely to consider others may be attributing their late arrival to personality or dispositional factors.

Although the surface-level dimension should be considered a good starting point for understanding and addressing challenging problems within educational settings, it is critical for educational leaders to look past the behaviors and actions of others and begin to consider the emotions and attitudes that fuel their actions. Emotions and feelings represent the below-the-surface dimension—the second dimension for educational leaders attempting to conceptualize problems in 3D.

Below-the-Surface Dimension

The below-the-surface dimension focuses on the role that emotions and feelings play in shaping the actions and behaviors of educators. Educational leaders should not only consider emotions and feelings when making decisions and problem solving. It also is essential they actively engage in conversations about feelings and emotions to ensure their understanding is both accurate and comprehensive. These conversations are critical because unexpressed feelings and emotions remain dormant and often bubble to the surface elsewhere.

Consider the situation at a small therapeutic high school that recently implemented a new cell phone policy. It was clear to the staff that student cell phone use was interfering with instruction and student learning. A decision was made to implement a new policy that required students to place their cell phones in locked pouches, where they would remain for the entirety of the school day. Teachers and staff had the ability to unlock the pouches when needed, but it was agreed by all that unlocking the pouches should be a rare exception during the school day. Although the faculty and staff expected a challenging transition period, they felt prepared to handle what behaviorists often refer to as the "extinction burst," when a behavior initially increases in frequency when reinforcement is removed.

Surprisingly, the transition to locked pouches went better than expected during the first two weeks. Student complaints were minimal, and the school leadership team did not receive any complaints from families. Many felt like the cell phone problem had been solved. Observations in classrooms soon proved otherwise. As it turns out, a majority of the students quickly figured out how to unlock, or more accurately break, the pouches. Most continued to take out their phones during classroom time, and teachers chose to avoid confrontations and continue with their lessons.

This example illustrates the distinction between public compliance and private acceptance, a second important concept from social psychology literature. Public compliance occurs when people "conform to other people's behavior publicly without necessarily believing in what they are doing or saying" (Aronson, Wilson, & Akert, 2010, p. 216). In contrast, private acceptance occurs when people "conform to other people's behavior out of a genuine belief that what they are doing or saying is right" (Aronson et al., 2010, p. 215). Although all teachers agreed cell phones were a problem, their behaviors and actions suggest support for using locked pouches as a solution was not universal. No one explicitly disagreed with the solution; however, the inconsistent enforcement of the new policy suggests many felt some form of pressure to publicly comply with the new approach. Consequently, their unexpressed feelings leaked out in their behaviors and actions, and the new cell policy failed. Similarly, although the students praised the new policy and went through the routine of locking their phones in pouches in the morning, they quickly began breaking those pouches and using their phones in the bathrooms and break areas.

Interestingly, when school staff came together again to discuss how the program was going, the first question posed to the group was "How are we all feeling about the new cell phone policy?" A teacher sitting in the back yelled out, "It sucks!" Laughter followed, but so did a meaningful conversation about the pouches and why the decision was made to utilize them in the first place. The leadership team invited feedback and facilitated conversation but also made a conscious attempt to listen to the teachers without interruption.

Some teachers felt the new policy was unreasonable; others felt that it was not strict enough. An interesting divide emerged between the middle and high school teacher teams. The program worked great in the middle school, and teachers did not want to lower expectations for students. Teachers talked about the importance of being consistent and shared that middle school students were locking up their phones or handing them in without incident. They also felt they were implementing the program with a high level of integrity by not allowing for exceptions or looking the other way when students attempted to access their phones. High school teachers, on the other hand, felt the problem was more complicated for the older students who were far more dependent on their phones and far less concerned about programmatic consequences. The discussion appeared to be heading in the direction of eliminating the cell phone policy for high school classrooms when one of the teachers stood up and exclaimed, "I still think we need the policy in place. I know it's hard, but these students cannot pay attention to their work when they have their phones, and the phones are creating way too many social problems that blow up in our face. My vote is to keep the policy, and we, the teachers, need to take it more seriously and not break when they begin to make our lives more complicated by begging to use their phones."

Ultimately, the group decided to continue to utilize the pouches, but, as a team, the high school teachers revamped the policy and restarted the implementation of the cell phone expectations. By giving teachers and staff an opportunity to express their feelings about and attitudes toward the new policy, the leadership team successfully brought the below-the-surface factors to the forefront in hopes of creating a more successful and durable solution to the cell phone problem.

Similarly, in the previous example regarding seating in the cafeteria, an exploration of student feelings uncovered that black and brown students often felt more comfortable and relaxed when sitting with their fellow students of color. White students expressed that they often did not feel close to the students of color because they rarely interacted with them in classes. These feelings uncovered a more challenging aspect of the cafeteria seating problem, and also revealed that many of the academic classes that were designed to be leveled by achievement and ability often resulted in classrooms that were racially segregated. This led to a far more important challenge for the district, one that required intervention at the systems-level.

Attitude inoculation is another important concept from social psychology literature that is helpful for school leaders who are introducing new interventions or programs to faculty and staff. Aronson et al. (2010) define attitude inoculation as "making people immune to attempts to change their attitudes by initially exposing them to small doses of the arguments against their position" (p. 194). In the cell phone example, capitalizing on this concept might have been extremely helpful for teachers struggling to enforce the new cell phone policy. If staff discussions included role-plays for how to respond to students when they break their pouches, take their phones out in class, or lie about not having a phone at all, teachers would be less likely to change their attitudes because they already had an opportunity to practice their responses to the students' anticipated behavior.

The role that emotions and feelings play in schools has increased exponentially over the last 25 years. Dozens of curricula have been introduced to educators, and social-emotional learning (SEL) is now becoming a priority for many educational leaders. The Collaborative for Academic and Social Emotional Learning (CASEL) has been a driving force for SEL programming across the country, and the 2011 landmark study (Durlak, Weissberg, Dymnicki, Taylor, & Schellinger, 2011) indicated that "SEL participants demonstrated significantly improved social and emotional skills, attitudes, behavior, and academic performance that reflected an 11-percentile-point gain in achievement" (p. 405). CASEL recommends that SEL curricula focus on self-awareness, self-management, responsible decision-making, and social awareness.

In his book *Permission to Feel* (2019), Dr. Marc Brackett shared data he obtained when he asked more than 5,000 teachers and 22,000 students to identify and report the emotions they felt each day. Seventy percent of teacher responses were negative and included responses such as "frustrated, overwhelmed, or stressed" (p. 191). Similarly, 77% of student responses were negative and included words like "tired, stressed, and bored" (p. 191). As educators, we cannot afford to ignore the powerful and informative feelings our teachers and students experience. This is why the below-the-surface dimension is so critical to our framework.

System Dimension

The system dimension, which encompasses the beliefs and values of an organization, plays a critical role in understanding problems and generating durable solutions. Unlike the first dimension (i.e., surface-level), which includes behaviors and actions, the system dimension is extremely difficult to observe directly and quantify. We can learn a great deal about the second dimension (i.e., below-the-surface) by asking direct questions about emotions and feelings to various stakeholders and, in turn, take their responses into consideration when developing programs or interventions to address specific challenges or problems. The complexity of the system dimension is far greater, and in many ways far more important, to understand when seeking to increase your influence as an educational leader.

During a recent consultation with a local school district, we were asked to observe a few of their programs at both the elementary and middle school levels for students with emotional and behavioral challenges. Students placed in the programs had been removed from traditional classroom environments for various reasons. Our first visit to the school district started with program observations at three different schools. Each observation lasted approximately 90 minutes, and, for the most part, we sat in the back of classrooms and/or program spaces when observing students and teachers. Thus, we were limited in our ability to truly understand problems, as we were only seeing what problems looked like above-the-surface (i.e., actions and behaviors of teachers and students). We learned that the majority of the students were males, classroom ratios were approximately one student per paraprofessional, program spaces were mostly isolated from mainstream classrooms and students, and students exhibited challenging and defiant behaviors that often were difficult to manage.

We then met with a small group of principals and assistant principals to hear more about the programs and their concerns for the students, teachers, and overall effectiveness of the programs themselves. These conversations were enlightening and allowed us to ask questions about the impact of these challenging students on learning environments throughout their buildings. The conversations were filled with emotions and feelings, and themes of frustration, stress, disappointment, and anger were palpable. These consistent below-the-surface symptoms were not limited to principals and assistant principals. They were equally present for teachers, students, parents, and families. As people became more willing to discuss their feelings and perceptions, a pattern emerged indicating part of the stress teachers and principals felt was related to the lack of support and understanding from district administrators. While district leaders supported the creation of the classes and staffing that went with the program, they seemed tone deaf to the toll the work was taking on service providers. A lack of understanding and lack of acknowledgment from district leaders about the emotional toll this work had on teaching staff led to anger and frustration among providers, which further zapped their energy.

One principal talked about how much time was spent working with police and family to locate a student who had run away. Instead of recognizing and appreciating the importance of these actions, he was criticized by district leaders for not getting his budget into central office on time that day. It was readily apparent to us that the district's current solution to the problem was not working—at least not to an extent that made key stakeholders happy. We began to shift our focus to the role of the system.

The system dimension is most often represented by school districts as a whole. Although there are times when officials from the Department of Education at the state level make decisions that directly influence local school districts (e.g., school closures during the COVID-19 pandemic or statewide assessment policies), we have found a majority of problems facing school districts exist within their respective systems. The system includes all members from each of the four stakeholder groups discussed in Chapter 1, as well as the interactions that take place within and between the four groups. Our approach to understanding the system within a school district has been influenced significantly by the work of Barry Oshry. Oshry (2007) emphasizes the importance of understanding the world of each stakeholder group and recommends Times Out of Time (TOOT) sessions, which include the following four basic guidelines for collecting information from sometimes tentative individuals within the system (p. 30):

1. Everyone Shows Up (All relevant parties must be part of the conversation.)
2. No Business (The purpose is to illuminate the system for all, not to problem solve.)
3. Tell the Truth (Paint a picture for us; you are our experts on your part of the system; there is no other way for us to know what your world is like.)
4. Listen Carefully to Others (Don't argue or debate; just let it in.)

Vignette—The Pizza Party

Mr. Rosen, an elementary school principal from a large suburban school district, was growing increasingly frustrated by the lack of efficiency he observed at the monthly staff meetings. Teachers often arrived late, left early, and rarely participated in group discussions. They spent more time paying attention to their laptops than the meeting itself and spent extended time in the parking lot debriefing the meeting in small groups. Mr. Rosen ultimately concluded staff meetings were unsuccessful because teachers were not as connected as they had been in the past. New teachers had been hired in recent years, veteran teachers had retired, and the group as a whole was not cohesive. He came up with what he thought was the perfect solution. He decided there would be no formal agenda at the next faculty meeting. He planned to order a bunch of pizzas and bring the group together to socialize with the goal of deepening relationships, which would ultimately repair the school's lack of connectedness.

On the day of the faculty meeting, Mr. Rosen made sure there was plenty of food and drinks for faculty and staff. He posted a simple agenda:

1. Take a break.
2. Have some lunch.
3. Mingle with your colleagues.
4. You Deserve It!

While some teachers arrived late, most stayed the entire meeting. They mingled some, but mostly remained in their grade-based teams. Mr. Rosen made sure he connected with each team and worked hard to avoid work-related topics. He felt the social event was a relative success and hoped the effects would manifest in meaningful ways in the coming weeks. His modest optimism was quickly crushed when second grade teacher Ms. Basquiat told him privately that many of the teachers complained about having to sit through two hours of "forced fun." They would have rather used the time to work on report cards in their classrooms.

Mr. Rosen felt frustrated and disappointed, more in himself than his teachers. He worked extremely hard, treated his teachers respectfully and fairly, was always understanding when they requested time off, and was supportive when they struggled with personal problems at home. Why was his team struggling to connect? Why did they appear to lack the level of investment he had seen in the past? Most importantly, what could he do as their leader to fix the problem?

Seeing the Problem in 3D

Mr. Rosen's challenge was a daunting one for sure, but not uncommon for school principals. His attempted solution was reasonable but limited in scope. He correctly identified the surface-level symptoms (e.g., his teachers were not engaged during staff meetings) and attributed those symptoms to his beliefs about the underlying problem (e.g., his staff was not connected). He then implemented a solution he believed would address the lack of connectedness. He failed to see the problem in a three-dimensional manner, however, which led to faulty conclusions and, ultimately, a solution that had little chance of success. Let's look at this problem through each of the three dimensions and see how the additional information would alter the potential solution.

Surface-Level Dimension

Mr. Rosen's frustration was due to teacher behaviors and actions during staff meetings. Teachers arrived late to meetings and often left early—behaviors which are easily observable. Further, teachers often worked on their computers during staff meetings and did not actively participate in discussion. Mr. Rosen viewed these behaviors as symptoms of an underlying problem. He attributed these actions and behaviors by teachers to a lack of connectedness and, therefore, created a solution to address the problem he identified. Educational leaders might get lucky in situations like these and correctly identify problems at first glance. Many times, however, this is not the case. Educational leaders run the risk of trying to solve the wrong problem when they fail to take time to consider the below-the-surface dimension. Consistent with the fundamental attribution error, Mr. Rosen incorrectly attributed the concerning behaviors to a lack of engagement.

Below-the-Surface Dimension

The second dimension focuses on the role feelings and attitudes play in challenging situations or problems. Mr. Rosen skipped this step, a common mistake for educational leaders who too often (a) feel pressure to solve problems quickly or (b) prefer to avoid more difficult conversations that might be hard to control. Challenging conversations that help leaders develop a better understanding of feelings and attitudes are critical, especially for leaders like Mr. Rosen, who are committed to improving their schools while simultaneously supporting teachers.

Mr. Rosen's pizza party was a reasonable first step toward establishing a plan to address his concerns. His meeting agenda needed to be modified, however. What if he had sent the following message to teachers and staff a week before the meeting?

> I'd like to propose an alternative format for the next staff meeting. We will provide pizza and refreshments for all teachers and staff. I'm hoping you will feel comfortable joining me in a conversation about how to improve our staff meetings. Although I take full responsibility for making our meetings as efficient and productive as possible, I've been having a hard time lately fulfilling this commitment to you and our school. Since I know that some of you feel more comfortable than others speaking in front of the group, I'd like to also provide you an alternative means of sharing your feedback and suggestions with me beforehand. Please feel free to return the enclosed card with comments prior to the meeting for me to review and integrate into our discussion. I look forward to our discussion. The card might include the following questions:
>
> 1. How do you feel about the staff meetings in general?
> 2. What personal factors should we spend more time discussing during our staff meetings?
> 3. What school-related or district-related factors should we spend more time discussing during our staff meetings?

An invitation to examine the problem as a school increases the likelihood of accurately identifying the "real" problem. Allowing teachers and staff to share their concerns publicly or privately makes it clear that he values everyone's perspective and their preferred approach of communicating their concerns. Communicating his goals in advance of the meeting allows others to reflect on the concerns and challenges they face, as well as how they want to articulate their concerns. This format steers the conversation away from behaviors and actions (e.g., late arrivals to meetings) toward feelings and attitudes (e.g., ways to improve staff meetings).

System Dimension

The third question given to teachers in advance widens the scope of the meeting to consider the system dimension. Since behaviors and actions are always part of the conversation, the first challenge is to integrate feelings and attitudes, which many educators are uncomfortable sharing. That is not sufficient, however. It also is imperative to consider the values and beliefs held by schools and/ or school districts. These represent the third dimension of seeing in 3D. Since the system dimension plays an active role in shaping the behaviors, actions, feelings, and attitudes of people within a system, viewing a problem through this lens is essential. Consider the following card Mr. Rosen received from one of his teachers.

> In response to Question 3, I find it very difficult to talk about anything other than the impending teacher strike due to the long-standing contract discussions within the district. There is so much pressure to stand united with the union, which is important to me. But I also struggle with the strained relationships I'm feeling with my students' families, as many of their parents are extremely upset with the teachers because of our actions and inactions.

This teacher's response communicates to the principal that strains within the overall system influences how she teaches (behaviors and actions) and, perhaps more importantly, how she feels about her teaching (feelings and attitudes). Her response allows Mr. Rosen to begin a conversation with staff about how district-wide stressors impact their teaching practices, as well as staff feelings and attitudes about coming to work and doing their jobs in the current climate. Ultimately, that might be the most important topic discussed during the staff meeting.

Much has been written about the importance of using data to inform decisions. We must expand our view of what constitutes data in order to include both the four perspectives described earlier and the three dimensions of dynamics that occur whenever people interact and communicate.

Examining a single meeting through these lenses can feel overwhelming at first. Given how many meetings educators attend during the course of a school year, it may make a deeper examination feel exhausting. Learning and practicing a new language or way of viewing things can be challenging initially. Our work in schools, however, has shown us that as people begin to use these lenses to better understand human dynamics, their vision expands beyond what is apparent to our eyes and ears. It is as if we begin to examine the stars with a powerful telescope. Our vision becomes sharper and clearer.

Taking in data from the four different perspectives, as well as the three dimensions, will deepen the understanding of problems or challenges facing educational leaders. This multi-layered understanding is critical to accurately diagnosing problems. Understanding is necessary but not sufficient to move forward and gain improvement. We believe there are four conditions or strategic leadership "moves" that create an eco-system where creative interventions develop alongside a commitment to their implementation. We will examine each of these conditions in Part II, Conditions for Change.

References

Aronson, E., & Aronson, J. (2018). *The social animal* (12th ed.). Worth Publishers.

Aronson, E., Wilson, T. D., & Akert, R. M. (2010). *Social psychology* (7th ed.). Pearson.

Brackett, M. (2019). *Permission to feel: Unlocking the power of emotions to help our kids, ourselves, and our society thrive.* Celadon Books.

Durlak, J. A., Weissberg, R. P., Dymnicki, A. B., Taylor, R. D., & Schellinger, K. B. (2011). The impact of enhancing students' social and emotional learning: A meta-analysis of school-based universal interventions. *Child Development, 82*(1), 405–432. doi:10.1111/j. 1467-8624.2010.01564.x.

Oshry, B. (2007). *Seeing systems: Unlocking the mysteries of organizational life* (2nd ed.). Berrett-Koehler Publishers.

Tatum, B. D. (2017). *Why are all the black kids sitting together in the cafeteria?: And other conversations about race* (Revised and updated). New York: Basic Books.

PART II

Conditions for Change

3

Balancing Psychological Safety with Accountability

Introduction

A therapeutic, alternative school was in lockdown after a teacher found a bullet in the stairwell. Staff members moved from classroom to classroom and searched all backpacks and bags. Caitlyn, a 15-year old junior, requested her bag be searched privately because police officers made her uncomfortable. She had reasons for wanting to avoid the search. Ultimately, a teacher and school counselor searched her bag. Inside was a full set of clothes, sneakers, makeup, and several other personal items, which raised eyebrows. Quick to explain, Caitlyn shared that she had run away from her group home the night before but was forced to return after being caught. Given the chaos of the lockdown, staff members decided to follow-up with Caitlyn at a later time.

Caitlyn later was dismissed from school and picked up by a caseworker from the group home. Distracted by the chaos of the lockdown and preparation for an afternoon presentation to the board of directors, first-year principal Mr. Heavey briefly spoke with Caitlyn and the caseworker and allowed them to leave. Three hours later, it was discovered that the man who picked Caitlyn up from school was not a caseworker at the group home. Rather, he was a probable sex trafficker en route to Florida with Caitlyn and two strangers in the back of his pickup truck. Mr. Heavey realized immediately he had not checked the man's ID at Caitlyn's dismissal. He called the police to report his concerns and met with them at the school minutes later. After providing police all information he had, Mr. Heavey offered any additional support necessary to find his student. As the search for Caitlyn continued, Mr. Heavey contacted the school superintendent, Dr. Kaplan, to inform her of the situation. Dr. Kaplan arrived at the school later that afternoon to meet with Mr. Heavey.

Mr. Heavey updated Dr. Kaplan on what they had learned about Caitlyn since the initial phone call. Police located her via her cell phone signal and felt confident she would be back at the group home within the hour. He summarized the day's events, including the discovery of a bullet, the lockdown, the backpack/bag search with police support, and his presentation to the board of directors. He continued, explaining how Caitlyn "claimed" she was being dismissed and his brief conversation with the man who picked her up from school. Finally, Mr. Heavey expressed disappointment and admitted he forgot to ask for the man's identification to verify he was a caseworker at the group home. Dr. Kaplan's immediate response was, "Why didn't you check his ID?" Mr. Heavey initially froze and then tried to explain, only to be cut off by the superintendent who said, "I'm sorry. I know the day was completely chaotic, and it was an oversight. We can talk more about the sequence of events tomorrow. For now, let's focus on what can we do next to support Caitlyn."

Some might judge the principal as incompetent for a number of reasons, but particularly because he endangered the safety of a student. By sharing this vignette, we hope to reflect on the importance of balancing psychological safety with accountability for educational leaders. It is easy to focus on accountability and consider whether to fire the principal or apply a punitive consequence such as putting a letter in his file or sending him home without pay. One also could overemphasize psychological safety and quickly see the principal's mistakes as completely understandable given the set of cir-cumstances and fact he is a novice leader. The school in this story is dedicated to students with significant emotional and behavioral challenges. Finding leaders to run these schools is not easy. Before examining the fallout from Mr. Heavey's decisions, it is important to understand what psychological safety is and why it is important in schools.

Defining Psychological Safety

Psychological safety is the primary need for groups to optimize their functioning. Amy Edmondson, Novartis Professor of Leadership and Management at Harvard Business School, identifies the importance of psychological safety for nimbleness needed to adapt successfully in a fast-paced world. People in organizations with sufficient psychological safety are more comfortable learning from mistakes, asking naïve questions, and recovering quickly from failures and setbacks. Equally important, however, is the role accountability plays for in-dividuals and groups who are part of the organization. When people or groups within an organization make mistakes or fail to meet goals, they need to take responsibility and, more im-portantly, learn from them so organizational evolution can take place. Therefore, balancing psychological safety and account-ability is imperative for positive cultural change.

"Psychological safety is broadly defined as a climate in which people are comfortable expressing and being themselves. More specifically, when people have psychological safety at work, they feel comfortable sharing concerns and mistakes without fear of embarrassment or retribution" (Edmondson, Kindle Locations, pp. 365–368). Educational leaders are re-sponsible for creating a climate that provides psychological safety for teachers and staff members. In doing so, they allow teachers to integrate innovative practices into their classrooms and share innovative practices with colleagues. Educators are more likely to share concerns when they believe they will be heard and considered. Similarly, educators are likely to share their mistakes when confident ensuing conversations will focus on lessons learned, rather than defending or justifying their actions.

Educators embrace the idea of creating classrooms and schools where students learn from their mistakes; yet they are reluctant to do that for themselves. Many grew up thinking professionalism means being an expert in one's craft and that expertise leaves little room for mistakes. While demands on teachers and educational leaders are great, a critical part of one's professional skill set is the ability to nimbly and continually learn and adapt. It is impossible to do that without experiencing a learning curve that involves mistakes and setbacks.

During the COVID-19 crisis, teachers transformed face-to-face teaching to distance learning. This was no simple feat and a far greater challenge than simply learning a new platform. Is it fair to expect perfection from these educators? What do we want from teachers facing this challenge? One hopes educators respond nimbly and use feedback and insight gained from the experience to continuously improve. Unfortunately, many schools lack such a culture and, therefore, could not adapt effectively to the crisis in a timely manner.

Assessing Psychological Safety

How do educational leaders assess whether or not their schools have psychological safety? Edmondson (2019) developed a questionnaire that numerous industries have adapted to assess their psychological safety. The prompts below have been adapted for educational leaders and schools.

1. If you make a mistake at school, it is often held against you.
2. Educators working at this school are able to bring up problems and tough issues.
3. Educators at this school sometimes reject others for being different.

4. It is safe to take a risk at this school.
5. It is difficult to ask other educators from this school for help.
6. No one at this school would deliberately act in a way that undermines my efforts.
7. Working with other educators from this school, my unique skills and talents are valued and utilized.

One challenge in assessing psychological safety with a survey is that educators in schools without psychological safety are unlikely to answer questions honestly. If responding teachers are concerned about how their answers will be interpreted or utilized, the survey will only be marginally helpful, at best. An alternative initial assessment of psychological safety requires educational leaders to conduct systematic observations of staff interactions and behaviors during numerous meetings and interactions throughout the school day. Staff meetings, team meetings, special education meetings, and department or grade-level meetings all present opportunities for educational leaders to assess psychological safety. We recommend using the following questions to guide such observations.

1. Do all participants share their "voices" during staff meetings or discussions?
2. Is the participant engagement fairly balanced across staff members?
3. How often do disagreements/arguments take place during staff meetings, and how are those disagreements processed?
4. When new initiatives are introduced at staff meetings, how often do teachers or staff members publicly voice concerns or objections?
5. How often are mistakes or failures discussed at staff meetings?
6. How often do teachers or staff members contribute to the meeting agenda? How often are they asked to contribute to the meeting agenda?

7. To what extent do the conversations in staff meetings continue afterwards in smaller groups?
8. How often are feelings and emotions part of the discussions during staff meetings?

The Power of Disagreements

Schools with a high level of psychological safety have little use for the default mantra, "Why can't we all just get along?" Teachers and staff are encouraged to consider and actively investigate alternative points of view. Instead of public compliance with the majority of faculty sitting on their hands and biting their lips, the goal becomes inner acceptance. Disagreements and conflict are encouraged, and influential school leaders are prepared to facilitate and participate in challenging conversations. A young principal in her third year at a new school shared the following story:

> We were wrapping up our monthly faculty meeting, which included a presentation of new professional development (PD) activities being offered by the district. After the presentation, I asked if anyone wanted to share their perspective or raise a question. One of my veteran teachers raised his hand and said, "I just want to share my frustration, and I think I speak for a lot of the teachers. These activities are overwhelming and do not feel important. We have given up a lot of our planning time, it's too confusing, and I'm not really sure what the benefits are to these PD activities." I knew right then that this was a critical point in my development as a school leader. We all sat in silence, and I thought carefully about how I wanted to respond to this question. Eventually, I responded, "Mr. Interrante, that must have been really hard for you to share. As a human being, it's also really hard for me to hear. But as someone who cares deeply about this school and all of our teachers, I want you to know that I really appreciate

your courage and willingness to give me honest and constructive feedback. We now can discuss these different perspectives. Thank you."

The principal's response was critical because it helped shape the school's climate by showing faculty it was safe, and even encouraged, to express disagreement and frustration in a professional and respectful way. The response validated the veteran teacher's concerns and set the stage for additional discussions to resolve problems inherent in the new PD proposals. Although validating the teacher's courage for bringing up a difficult topic was essential in that moment, the problem-solving conversations and efforts that followed were equally important, as psychological safety does not translate to perpetual agreement.

Psychological Safety and Cognitive Dissonance

In the preceding example, the principal was placed in a difficult position. Her decision to implement a new set of PD options she believed to be in the best interest of students and teachers was challenged by teachers resistant to the change and questioning her rationale. The principal experienced what social psychologists refer to as cognitive dissonance.

Festinger (1957) defines cognitive dissonance as "a state of tension that occurs whenever an individual simultaneously holds two cognitions (ideas, attitudes, beliefs, opinions) that are psychologically inconsistent" (p. 110). Stated differently, two cognitions are dissonant if, when considered alone, the opposite of one follows from the other. For the third-year principal, the dissonant cognitions include:

1. I think it is important we adapt these new PD offerings to meet the academic and social-emotional needs of our students, and I know it is extremely important to the administration team in the district.
2. I want my teachers to like me and believe in me as the leader of the school, but they oppose the new PD offerings.

The principal is faced with the daunting challenge to reduce dissonance, as are the teachers. The conflicting cognitions of the teachers are likely different, however, and may include:

1. I want more ownership of our PD and do not see any reason why we should do these administrator-driven offerings. These new strategies mean more work for me.
2. The principal is my boss, and she makes the final decision. As our new leader, I want to be supportive of new initiatives.

Social psychology literature includes three basic ways people can reduce cognitive dissonance. First, people can change their behavior so it aligns with the dissonant cognition. In this example, teachers can start actively supporting the new PD proposals to increase the likelihood they will be successful. Or perhaps the principal can eliminate or reduce the offerings to increase the likelihood her teachers will like her. Second, people can alter the dissonant cognition so it justifies their behavior. For example, the teachers might reconsider the benefits of the new proposals and recognize that although the transition might be difficult at first, it will be worthwhile in the end. Similarly, the principal might revise how important it is to be liked by her teachers, placing greater priority on doing what is best for the students and families. Finally, people can add new cognitions to justify their behaviors. Teachers might add, "We get a new principal every three years, so it's not worth jumping through all of these hoops to support her when she's going to leave soon." The principal's new cognition might be, "I know professional development is important, but I could have introduced it to the faculty in a different way to increase their buy-in. Perhaps I can put things on hold for now and invite teachers to help me revise the PD offerings for the following school year."

School communities that truly value and foster psychological safety become more comfortable with cognitive dissonance over time. Community members learn feelings of dissonance are expected and reveal disagreements that must be understood and considered in order for the system to evolve and improve.

For the novice principal, this means revisiting how the PD offerings were introduced initially and how that process can be revised moving forward to increase teacher participation. For the teachers, this means recognizing the leadership has changed. Hopefully, the new principal is open to feedback and willing to incorporate it into new practices at the school.

Feedback Loops and Psychological Safety

Psychological safety plays a critical role in feedback and evaluation cycles. A new administrator at a therapeutic program for students with emotional and behavioral challenges brought to our attention that teachers were growing increasingly frustrated by school counselors. Teachers complained that services were not delivered in compliance with Individual Education Plans (IEPs), parent outreach was insufficient or absent altogether, and counselors were not communicating with teachers about educationally-relevant discussions during sessions. After several conversations with both teachers and the program director, the obvious questions were, "How have counselors responded to these complaints? What is their side of the story?" Unfortunately, difficult conversations never took place. The concerns of teachers were never shared directly with counselors, and counselors were never given an opportunity to explain their actions or improve. Teachers felt resentful and dissatisfied with counselors because nothing changed. Counselors were unaware a problem existed.

A lack of authentic discussions about how to improve clinical supports in the program, as well as the generic and overwhelmingly positive annual reviews counselors received, suggest an imbalance between psychological safety and accountability. Edmondson would say the program operated in the *Comfort Zone,* meaning the level of psychological safety was high but the standards for professional practice were low.

For improvement to occur, school leaders must work hard to balance a high level of psychological safety and professional standards (i.e., accountability). Under these conditions, teachers are well prepared and expect to hear constructive feedback. In psychologically-safe environments, people experience honest and specific feedback and are provided needed support to grow and improve. If improvement over time does not occur, people are held accountable through a range of evaluative consequences. Evidence of improvement and the extent of learning would be parts of the annual review meetings and an integral part of the school culture. Teachers would actively share and discuss both their successes, to promote positive practices, as well as their failures, so all teachers can learn from their mistakes. Constructive feedback, however, is not only important for teachers but for educational leaders as well.

To balance psychological safety with accountability, leaders must develop two-way feedback channels. Accountability must go in both directions—toward and from both teachers and leaders. In schools, principals provide feedback to educators on their teaching and direct service to students. In psychologically-safe environments, educators would also provide feedback to leaders about their leadership. This bi-directional flow of feedback enriches the data and information available to support continuous improvement. Additionally, for feedback loops to be effective and authentic, consideration and assignment of blame must be removed from the environment in order to maximize learning. Blame leads to punishment, but punishment does not engender deep learning.

Edmondson (2019) discusses the importance of *blameless reporting* related to psychological safety using an example from Children's Hospital and Clinics in Minneapolis, Minnesota. The Chief Operating Officer (COO) of the hospital introduced a new policy called blameless reporting—"a system inviting confidential reports about risks and failures people observed" (Edmondson, 2019, Kindle Location, p. 3691). The COO, Ms. Julie Morath, intentionally used language in an attempt to maximize learning opportunities following errors. She spoke of "accidents" and "failures" instead of errors. When mistakes were made in patient treatment and care, employees were guaranteed no negative consequences. This was a sharp departure from the traditional approach where an investigation

Safe Spaces	Brave Spaces
Prioritize politeness	Prioritize honesty and authenticity
Value comfort when discussing difficult issues	Acknowledge discomfort as inevitable in discussion of difficult issues
Can lead to defensiveness and deflection	Value risk taking, vulnerability, and being challenged
Narrowly define safety, usually stemming from a dominant perspective	Contend that safety means different things to different people and groups
Tend not to prepare participants for difficult conversations	Prepare groups for difficult conversations

TABLE 3.1   Difference Between Safe and Brave Spaces

could lead to punishment. Medical staff rarely make errors on purpose. Mistakes and failures typically are not individual ones, but systemic. Children's Hospital hoped blameless reporting would enable supervisors to determine root causes of mistakes in order to prevent repeating them. Equally important, hospital healthcare professionals learned to expect conversations about accidents or failures related to patient safety.

Similarly, culture shifts are critical for schools looking to implement effective and authentic feedback loops. By placing the focus on student learning and successful student experiences within classrooms and schools, teachers and educational leaders must increase their comfort level with both giving and receiving feedback. Transitions are challenging and require educators to be willing to participate in difficult and brave conversations. The benefits for educational leaders, teachers and, most importantly, students are well worth the work needed to create a psychologically-safe school environment.

Psychological Safety Is Not a Timid Space

Psychological safety does not mean everyone is nice to each other at all times. That is far from accurate. Psychologically-safe environments can be challenging because they are designed to encourage honest and direct questions, comments, and feedback. Such behaviors produce discomfort at times. Many find it difficult to be direct at meetings when people with authority and power present. Navigating a psychologically-safe culture requires a certain level of courage, especially at the beginning. Timid people will feel uncomfortable, at first. Psychologically-safe spaces require bravery on the part of participants. Table 3.1 outlines the differences between safe and brave spaces Araro Landreman 2013 (Araro & Clemens, 2013).

Putting the Balance into Practice

Dr. Kaplan has a difficult decision to make in response to the challenging events that took place in Mr. Heavey's program. The notion of supporting Mr. Heavey might feel inappropriate or lacking in judgment to some, as his lapse in judgment endangered the safety of a student. That perspective is worthy of conversation and consideration. But punishing or firing Mr. Heavey clearly emphasizes accountability over psychological safety. Will punishing or firing Mr. Heavey lead to improved student safety, or will it simply result in increasing levels of staff anxiety and insecurity? Edmondson describes how environments can become "Anxiety Zones," resulting in "employees (who) are anxious about speaking up, and both work quality and workplace safety suffer" (Kindle Locations, pp. 794–795). Occasionally, infractions and poor decisions in schools certainly warrant harsh and immediate consequences, especially if the consequence increases the safety of the school. If a teacher hits a student, a coach is emotionally abusive, or an educator demonstrates a pattern of poor decisions despite clear and constructive feedback, immediate and decisive action would be justified. In the case of Mr. Heavey, however, the balance between psychological safety and accountability suggests additional conversation is necessary for the superintendent to make an informed decision.

It would be important to discuss the sequence of events with Mr. Heavey and learn from his reflections and insights. In the blameless reporting protocol referenced in Edmondson's book, the CEO recommended asking healthcare employees "Was everything as safe as you would like it to have been this week with your patients" (Kindle Location, pp. 3681–3682) to gain insights and improve patient care. In Mr. Heavey's case, the question might be "Was everything as safe as you would like it to have been on Tuesday with your teachers and students?" Mr. Heavey then would be able to detail where his decisions, judgments, and actions broke down, as well as the effective steps he took to support Caitlyn. Dr. Kaplan likely would feel he learned from the experience and has become a stronger leader as a result of what he learned from his mistakes. Through discussion and reflection, Mr. Heavey and Dr. Kaplan also can identify action items that would ultimately increase student safety during times of crisis and for students in similar situations as Caitlyn.

Educational leaders must decide to develop a culture of learning and continuous improvement. To do that, we must pursue the goal of balancing psychological safety with accountability. This means breaking from a tradition of punishing people for mistakes and replacing it with a culture that recognizes mistakes will be made and improvement emerges when we learn from them.

References

Araro, B., & Clemens, K. (2013). From safe spaces to brave spaces: A new way to frame dialogue around diversity and social justice. In L. M. Landreman (Ed.), *The art of effective communication: Reflections from social justice educators* (pp. 135–150). Stylus Publishing.

Edmondson, A. C. (2019). *The fearless organization: Creating psychological safety in the workplace for learning, innovation, and growth.* Wiley and Sons.

Festinger, L. (1957). *A theory of cognitive dissonance.* Amsterdam University Press.

Rozovsky, J. (November 17, 2015). *The five keys to a successful Google team.* Re: Work Blog. Retrieved from https://rework.withgoogle.com/blog/five-keys-to-a-successful-google-team/P.

4

Strengthening Belonging

Introduction

In his book *The Culture Code*, Daniel Coyle discusses the importance of belonging. He writes that belonging cues are behaviors that create safe connections in groups. They include proximity, eye contact, energy, mimicry, turn taking, attention, body language, vocal pitch, consistency of emphasis, and whether everyone talks to everyone else in the group. Like any language, belonging cues cannot be reduced to an isolated moment but, rather, consist of a steady pulse of interactions within a social relationship. They seek to answer ever-present questions in the back of our minds: Are we valued here? What is our future with these people? Does my voice count?

The importance of belonging cannot be understated in schools, as a strong sense of belonging transforms into the energy needed for improvement and helps create a vibrant, supportive learning community. A weak sense of belonging among staff members can foster resentment and divisiveness, lead to frequent burnout and high teacher turnover, and drain desperately-needed energy. How can educational leaders assess the sense of belonging present in their schools? What can they do to strengthen the sense of belonging when it appears to be fractured or lacking? The following provides an overview of belonging and principles used to create and maintain strong connections among educators, as well as common indicators and pitfalls to be mindful of when attempting to create a strong sense of belonging within schools and school districts.

Group Cohesiveness

Aronson, Wilson, and Akert (2010) use the term *group cohesiveness* rather than a sense of belonging and suggests that there are qualities of a group that bind members together and promote liking between members. The more cohesive a group, the more likely they are to remain in the group, take part in activities, and try to recruit like-minded members to join. Aronson et al. states that when a task requires close cooperation between group members, such as a football team executing a difficult play, cohesiveness helps performance. Interestingly, when maintaining good relations among group members seems more important than finding good solutions to problems, cohesiveness can get in the way of optimal performance. In schools, this means maintaining good relationships with colleagues and families may actually serve as a deterrent for improvement and innovative programming. The challenge educational leaders face is building a foundation for learning that fosters a sense of belonging that is not compromised by conflict and disagreement.

Given the examples from Aronson et al., school leaders can assess the sense of belonging, or group cohesiveness, present in their schools by observing the following:

- ◆ What is the daily attendance rate of the staff?
- ◆ What is the retention rate of the staff?
- ◆ What stories do people tell about their work culture?
- ◆ How often do we hear from all voices at a meeting?
- ◆ How often do teachers or staff members attempt to recruit others to join the staff?
- ◆ How often do teachers or staff members offer support and guidance to one another?

Although not an exhaustive list of questions, these six questions can inform educational leaders if their teachers and staff members experience a sense of belonging that promotes a positive and supportive school culture. While contemplating the answers to the first set of questions, educational leaders should also ask themselves the following:

◆ Am I providing a variety of meaningful growth and service opportunities that are considerate of my teachers' and staff members' needs?

◆ Am I structuring my staff meetings in a way that invites engagement in a manner that respects their time, seeks their perspectives, and listens deeply to their suggestions and feedback?

◆ How am I supporting my teachers and staff members so they feel comfortable navigating the recommendations provided for their growth and improvement?

◆ What am I doing to make sure my teachers and staff members feel appreciated and connected to the school so they will want to remain part of the team?

◆ What am I doing to actively encourage, support, and recognize collegiality among my teachers and staff members?

The second set of questions likely feels more empowering, as you are identifying ways to increase belonging by taking personal responsibility for how certain things are structured within the school environment. Belonging is not a static variable. Rather, it is a dynamic, interactive variable that can be strengthened by strong leadership.

Social Norms and Core Values

Social norms and core values are two additional indicators of belonging. Surprisingly, many teachers and staff members are not aware of the social norms or core values at their schools, although many regularly see them posted in school lobbies or on backs of meeting agendas. Equally important to identifying social norms and core values is how they are (a) developed and communicated to all teachers and staff members at the school and (b) used to drive the desired culture.

Social norms are "the implicit or explicit rules a group has for the acceptable behaviors, values, and beliefs of its members" (Aronson et al., 2010, p. 222). Common examples of explicit social norms include sharing the floor during school meetings, listening respectively, reserving judgment, and assuming good intentions. It is important for school leaders to recognize explicit social norms often are different than implicit ones. A common implicit social norm for school-based teams uncomfortable with conflict may be "everyone must get along." When this is the implicit social norm, group members avoid disagreements and/ or voicing opposing perspectives to avoid conflict. Doing so may avoid conflict, but it also restricts team growth and, ultimately, limits a team's effectiveness to teach and support students. This is known as *normative social influence.*

We have noticed educators who use norms more often rely on establishing what we describe as *technical norms.* Technical norms focus on the visible aspects of a meeting (Chapter 2). Technical norms include starting and ending meetings on time and the process for shaping the agenda. Often left out of technical norms are expectations around engagement and conflict. These norms are adaptive in nature. Examples of adaptive norms include:

- We are willing to engage in conflict and stay engaged to resolution.
- We will lean into discomfort.
- We will take responsibility for identifying what is troubling us and sharing it with the appropriate person.
- We will listen for the quiet voice and reach out to those who are slow to speak in groups.

Adaptive norms focus on the less visible, yet still impactful, dimensions of meetings. While meetings benefit from both technical and adaptive norms, established norms will have little impact on the effectiveness of meetings without regular assessment. Assessing norms is another way to balance psychological safety with accountability (Chapter 3). While norms are designed to foster safety, we also know there will be violations. Leaders hold participants and themselves accountable for adherence to norms by having groups assess their "norm performance." We recommend a very simple norm assessment. At the end of each meeting, participants simply fill out a Likert prompt such as "To what degree did I follow our group's norms?" or "To what degree did our group follow the norms?" There are times when individuals assess their norm performance as very good but not the group's performance. That contrast in assessment can form the basis for a very rich discussion at the next meeting.

Normative Social Influence and Belonging

Normative social influence is "the influence of other people that leads us to conform in order to be liked and accepted by them" (Aronson et al., 2010, p. 222). They continue, "This type of conformity results in public compliance with the group's beliefs and behaviors but not necessarily private acceptance of those beliefs and behaviors." Normative social influence has been investigated since the landmark Asch line judgment experiment almost 70 years ago (1951). In the experiment, participants were shown two boxes. One box had a single line drawn in it; the other had three lines of varying lengths. The participants were asked to point to the line in the second box that was the same length as the single line in the first box. When the participants were alone, they almost always chose the correct line. The study's primary contribution, however, came when the participants were asked to choose the correct line when in a group where all other members intentionally chose the wrong line. Astonishingly, 76% of the participants conformed to the group and selected the wrong line at least once during the experiment. Their need to be accepted by the group was clearly more important than their need to be correct. The implications of this for school-based teams are extraordinary.

Picture a TEAM meeting for a child recently evaluated for a specific learning disability (SLD). The school-based team and the child's family sit around a conference table and begin to work their way through the special education eligibility flowchart. The very first question asks, "Does the student have one or more of the following types of disability?" The team chair concludes that based on the completed evaluations, the student does not have a disability. Members of the school-based team and family are then asked if they agree with that determination. Head nods make their way around the table until they reach the classroom teacher who has been struggling with the student throughout the school year. Although the teacher feels strongly the student needs additional support and suspects the student does, indeed, have a learning disability, he feels uncomfortable disagreeing with the group and ultimately decides not to share his perspective. He nods his head in agreement instead—much like choosing the wrong line in the Asch line experiment despite knowing the correct answer.

Asch extended the study in two important ways, both of which have clear implications for school leaders. In the first condition, the investigator had one group member disagree with other group members prior to the participant making their selection. In this scenario, conformity decreased dramatically. In the second condition, participants were asked to write down their selections rather than reporting them aloud in front of the group. Once again, conformity decreased dramatically. In both cases, the researcher identified specific strategies that can be utilized to counteract the power of normative social influence. The Asch line study focused on understanding the social influences that foster conformity. One theory to explain participants choosing incorrect responses is normative social influence. A second possible explanation is informational social influence.

Informational Social Influence and Belonging

Informational social influence is "the influence of other people that leads us to conform because we see them as a source of information to guide our behavior" (Aronson et al., 2010, p. 215). They continue, "We conform because we believe that others' interpretation of an ambiguous situation is more correct than ours and will help us choose an appropriate course of action." Just as the Asch line experiment demonstrated the power of normative social influence, the landmark experiment for informational social influence is the Milgram Study of Compliance (1964).

In Milgram's experiment, participants were placed in the role of a "teacher" and asked to administer word association tasks to a "learner," who was a confederate of the experimenter. When the learner responded incorrectly, the teacher was told to administer electric shocks to the learner at increasing levels of intensity ranging from "Slight Shock" (15–60 volts) to "Danger: Severe Shock" and "XXX" (375–450 volts). Amazingly, more than 60% of the participants in the experiment delivered shocks to the learner all the way to the end of the lesson, including the 450-volt shock (Aronson et al., 2010). The goal of the experiment was to understand the conditions that led people to obey authority figures. Milgram concluded that participants followed the orders of the expert authority figure because they did not feel personally responsible, the experiment was fast-paced in nature, and the shock levels increased in small increments (Aronson et al., 2010). Although informational social influence helps explain obedience, the compliant behaviors that follow are strongly associated with public compliance rather than private acceptance (Chapter 4). Disrupting public compliance requires addressing problems within the school climate that result in educators being hesitant to disagree with one another or challenge authority figures within the school, common symptoms of the culture of "nice" (MacDonald, 2011).

Culture of Nice

MacDonald (2011) explains a culture of "nice" is one where educators feel deeply reluctant to openly critique their own instructional practices or those of others. This serves as a barrier to thoughtful, meaningful sharing, especially in professional learning community (PLC) contexts. Teachers tend to only say nice things about the work of others, even when the goal is to improve practice. MacDonald shares signs the culture of "nice" may be creeping into your professional conversation:

- Teachers rarely question each other's and their own practice, assumptions, and beliefs.
- Teachers only share successful student work to avoid judgment from peers.
- Teachers who share their unsuccessful student work and those examining it make excuses as to why the student underperformed.
- Teachers recommend strategies for the presenting teacher to apply, but don't critically reflect and apply them to their own instruction.

MacDonald offers specific strategies to refocus discussion in a more critical, honest direction. The goal, she argues, is to replace the culture of nice with a culture of trust—where teachers feel safe sharing their own growth areas and those of their students. MacDonald recommends establishing group norms that allow teachers to recognize when discussion has shifted to "nice" and actively redirect it back to a more self-reflective approach. Another suggestion is to focus on the learning dilemma students are encountering rather than the teacher themselves. Finally, MacDonald encourages PLC facilitators to debrief each PLC session, specifically challenging teachers to reflect on how authentic, critical, and self-reflective their discussion was.

MacDonald's article echoes powerful points made by Richard Elmore and his colleagues in their work on instructional rounds. Until teachers and principals can separate the personal from the practice, meaningful growth in practice—and in student achievement—will be limited. School leaders bear a key responsibility for confronting the culture of nice and fostering a culture of honesty and ongoing professional growth in its place.

Five Dysfunctions of a Team—Lencioni

Author and former Bain consultant Patrick Lencioni links safety and openness to different perspectives to the overall effectiveness teams. In his book *The Five Dysfunctions of a Team* (2002), Lencioni provides insights into the hierarchy of needs groups must meet to embrace and pursue goals until desired results are achieved. The first need Lencioni describes is trust.

Sufficient trust is established when members of a team are able to mention at meetings the setbacks and challenges they are facing, including the mistakes and failures that are an inevitable part of creating a new strategy or achieving a high-quality goal. Trust is not necessarily present simply because people feel good about each other. Trust means we can share experiences and examples when we might not have performed in the way we had hoped. Once sufficient trust is achieved, the next need to meet is overcoming fear of conflict.

Some people are comfortable dealing with conflict with colleagues. Others find it uncomfortable and potentially damaging to relationships, so they avoid it at all costs. In the book *Flawless Consulting*, Peter Block wrote, "There is a prevailing belief that in order to get ahead, we must be cautious in telling the truth" (2011, p. 117). Lencioni's work suggests that unless a team is willing to "rumble," their commitment to the work (i.e., the goals) will be insufficient. We have experienced many meetings in schools where controversial issues are brought up, but diverging faculty perspectives are not openly communicated. Leaders sometimes interpret the absence of disagreement as a sign that they can move forward only to find out later the policy that was "approved" was not actually embraced. Lencioni teaches us that without a good fight, there is no commitment. Insufficient commitment means stakeholders will not hold themselves accountable when results are inadequate. As with the cell phone policy discussed earlier, students did not follow the new policy, nor did the teachers follow through when they observed students disregarding the new policy. While no new policy or goal is implemented or achieved easily, people will respond differently when they see a violation or a lack of achievement when they have been actively involved in creating the expectation. It will bother them because they are committed to the goal. If stakeholders are not willing to hold themselves accountable, there will be (in Lencioni's words) "inattention to results."

Belonging in Action—Solving the Cafeteria Problem

Following the excitement of being hired as a middle school principal, a consultee of ours was surprised by the repeated well wishes from his soon-to-be faculty and the recurring comment, "Hopefully you can finally fix the cafeteria problem!" Despite being hired to take on a leadership position within an affluent and extremely high-achieving school district, the persistent pleas of teachers kept going back to the out of control, disrespectful, and wild behaviors of students during lunchtime. More than 80 students daily opted to eat elsewhere or sought refuge in the nurse's office because behavior problems were persistent and disruptive in the cafeteria. The 300+ students who did find their way to the cafeteria would sit wherever they wanted. Bullying and exclusive behaviors occurred. Powerful students made it difficult for less powerful students to find a seat. Teachers on lunch duty only knew a few students by name because there were so many in each lunch period. Consequently, it was challenging for them to hold students accountable for cleaning up their lunch tables before exiting the cafeteria. Social psychology has taught us diffusion of responsibility can be a recipe for poor behavior. Thus, lunch was seen as "hell on earth" dreaded by most teachers and students.

The new principal took a few months to develop core values with his faculty. Developing a deep respect for one another and the school building was one of the values. Being able to learn from mistakes was another. The principal knew core values were tools to help solve problems. Once values were established, he assembled a team of teachers to take on pressing issues in the cafeteria. It was clear to members of the committee that behavior in the cafeteria violated most of the core values. As the committee started to examine the problem, it quickly became apparent not knowing students' names made it difficult to maintain respect and decorum during lunchtime. To ensure all students acted responsibly, teachers needed to know the names of students. To do that required assigned seats. Ugh! No one wanted to inform students of this policy change. People feared there would be enormous backlash from both students and parents, who were told by previous administrators that lunchtime was an opportunity for students to make friends and mingle with students from all parts of town. The principal pointed out one of their core values was learning from their mistakes. While it may take time to get the system right, the school should move ahead with the change.

It was not an easy transition. Students balked; parents complained. But once the decision was made, guided by the core values of the school, adults started to participate more fully. Cafeteria staff decided to change lunch options and offered students more choices. Custodial staff made peg boards that held dust pans and brushes numbered to coordinate with table numbers, which allowed students to clean up more efficiently. Lunch supervisors now knew who sat at each table, which enabled them to assign clean up duties and, if necessary, call students back to the cafeteria if they did not do their jobs. Little by little, lunch supervision became more tolerable, and students worried less about finding a seat in a large cafeteria. These ideas were founded on a set of core values. Without core values, the principal would not have been able to succeed.

Students are not fully present and focused on their learning without a sense of belonging. This axiom also applies to educators. Creating a sense of belonging is complex, as leaders must assess where belonging falls short and take action to increase the sense of safety and the sense that all voices matter. Norms and values must be authentic, regularly assessed, and provide the assurances people need to feel their voices matter, even when they might have a different point of view. Not all students felt safe in the cafeteria or that they belonged there during lunch. Adults dreaded being there as well. Principals do not take courses in how to improve belonging in school cafeterias. Figuring out root problems and addressing them in iterative steps requires multiple perspectives thinking through what might be blocking or limiting the sense of belonging so critical to learning.

References

Aronson, E., Wilson, T. D., & Akert, R. M. (2010). *Social psychology* (7th ed.). Pearson.

Block, P. (2011). *Flawless consulting: A guide to fetting your expertise used* (3rd ed.). Pfeiffer.

Lencioni, P. (2002). *The five dysfunctions of a team: A leadership fable* (1st ed.). Jossey-Bass.

MacDonald, E. (2011). When nice won't suffice: Honest discourse is key to shifting school culture. *Journal of Staff Development, 32*(3), 45–47.

Milgram, S. (1964). Group pressure and action against a person. *The Journal of Abnormal and Social Psychology, 69*(2), 137–143. doi:10.1037/h0047759.

5

Engaging in Open and Honest Communication

Introduction

One of the best communication tools we have seen is a ping-pong table at a nearby therapeutic program for high school students. Educators there believe students need breaks and social opportunities. Going to the game room and playing ping-pong does not need to be earned. Rather, it is built into student schedules like math and history. To be clear, students do not spend equal time playing ping-pong and learning about math and history. Teachers are also skilled at ping-pong, which sets up some competitive matchups and fierce battles. When games include students who are not evenly matched, the final scores are often blowouts. Better players usually have serves few can return, and games are often over before less skilled players even get a chance to serve. After their best serve sails over the net, the stronger player smashes it back into the corner of the table—and the rout is on. Weaker players figure out quickly that ping-pong might not be their game—unlikely to try again because their first experiences were not positive ones.

Fortunately, an alternative version of ping-pong emerged after a high school freshman asked a classmate, "Let's see how long we can volley without the ball hitting the ground?" A simple suggestion, but a drastic paradigm shift. The two students took turns starting volleys, paying careful attention to what was easier for the other student to return. As they became more comfortable with one another and trusted their respective abilities to keep volleys going, the shots slowly increased in speed and hit counts began to accumulate more quickly. Students celebrated their accomplishments together and began posting "records" on a whiteboard in the game room.

The new game shifted the objective from dominating and winning to working towards a shared goal. Cooperation replaced competition. More importantly, many students became better players because of the new game. Many students previously not playing ping-pong started to join the fun. This is what needs to take place in schools to establish a culture that fosters open and honest communication. Team discussions and district-wide meetings cannot be dominated by more vocal, aggressive, or powerful participants. Challenging topics must be investigated from different perspectives, and varied opinions should be valued, explored, and genuinely considered. Open and honest communication transforms school communities and fosters healthy and adaptive development for all educators. Lessons drawn from social and organizational psychology hold implications for school leaders looking to foster positive communication practices.

In their seminal article about school culture, Saphier and King (1985) identified open and honest communication as one of the essential norms of a vibrant learning community. Amy Edmondson identified open and honest discussions at meetings as a key indicator of psychological safety (Chapter 3), which is one of the essential components of a culture focused on learning. It is critical for educational leaders to develop conditions and habits that encourage talking openly and honestly about concerns or reactions to ideas and initiatives, regardless of power differentials among individuals. For many, this seems impossible. The fear to share questions and criticisms openly in many schools and organizations is palpable and difficult to overcome. There is often deep worry that honest conversations will jeopardize job security or limit our capacity to survive and thrive in school environments. Yet, the perspectives, ideas, and questions educators have are an incredibly important source of data for educational leaders. When open and honest communication is missing, educational leaders make decisions and shape school practices and routines based on incomplete data and limited understanding of the true wants and needs of the system. Following are contributions from several notable researchers, along with our collective experiences as educators and consultants, that will help educational leaders foster open and honest communication practices in their schools.

Minimizing the Nondiscussables

One primary obstacle to open and honest communication is the presence of nondiscussables within a school community. Barth (2002) defined nondiscussables as "subjects sufficiently important that they are talked about frequently but are so laden with anxiety and fearfulness that these conversations take place only in the parking lot, the restrooms, the playground, the car pool, or the dinner table at home" (p. 6). Common nondiscussables in schools include how decisions are made, leadership style of principals, critiques of certain teaching practices, inconsistent expectations or treatment of teachers and staff members, conflict involving teacher unions, and issues related to race. Barth offered an important metric for assessing the health of a school culture saying, "The health of a school is inversely proportional to the number of nondiscussables: the fewer nondiscussables, the healthier the school; the more nondiscussables, the more pathology in the school culture" (p. 7).

Barth's insights about nondiscussables are not just abstract ideas. There are concrete examples of nondiscussables in most schools, which need to be acknowledged and addressed by educational leaders so communication and educational practices can be examined and improved over time. Open and honest communication is connected powerfully to psychological safety.

Educational leaders must work hard to identify and acknowledge nondiscussables in their schools and drag them out into the open for discussion and problem-solving. Understanding how nondiscussables become invisible and unapproachable in the first place is important.

Power Differentials

Edmondson (2019) explains how perceived power differentials at NASA resulted in cultural conditions that did not support the open exchange of information. She discusses how a NASA engineer believed he had observed a technical difficulty during a shuttle launch-day video and was interested in securing additional footage to learn more about the potential malfunction. His concerns were largely dismissed by his superiors, and, ultimately, the Space Shuttle Columbia disintegrated upon re-entry into the Earth's atmosphere. Results of a subsequent investigation supported the engineer's initial concerns and determined the tragic deaths of crew members aboard the shuttle might have been preventable. When the engineer was asked why he failed to speak up, his response was typical of an employee who had learned to accept his position in the organizational hierarchy. He was not comfortable challenging authority figures positioned on rungs higher up the ladder. Edmondson concludes her NASA story by acknowledging the challenges associated with speaking up but also saying, "The higher ups in a position to listen and learn are often blind to the silencing effects of their presence" (Kindle Location 2064). Her statement resonates with our experiences consulting with school leaders and leadership teams and contributes to our desire to write this book for educational leaders. These leaders are in position to change school cultures by appreciating their influence and empowering teachers and staff to speak up and be heard.

Power differentials in schools result in educators failing to speak up every day. For example, new teachers are reluctant to share their impressions of the new math curriculum; social workers stay quiet about their concerns with the new social emotional learning (SEL) curriculum, the third one in four years; or an IT director with concerns about the security of a new meeting platform opts not to speak up because of a lack of familiarity with the new superintendent. In each situation, power differentials serve as barriers to open and honest communication. Opportunities to improve the system and school environment are missed because members of the community do not feel comfortable sharing their opinions, lacking confidence that their voices are valued by those in positions of power.

There are numerous power differentials in schools to consider beyond the obvious authority gap between principals and teachers. Power differences exist between senior staff and less experienced teachers, as well as teachers and teaching assistants. These differentials can hinder communication between departments within school districts as well, such as the divide between special education and regular education resources, or teachers from the math and history departments at a high school. Special educators or student service providers often feel their voices are diminished due to their smaller caseloads and different responsibilities than regular education teachers. Wellness and fine arts teachers often feel less important than traditional academic teachers. Unstated, but strong, beliefs about the importance of certain subject matter can assign different values to the voices of educators. Part-time educators often struggle to find their voices, even if they are actually full-time employees assigned to multiple schools within a district.

Power differentials also exist based on social capital within a school building or district. Teachers with louder voices tend to dominate staff discussions and influence the direction of conversation. In many of our consultations with principals and other school leaders, a common complaint revolves around limiting the participation of specific teachers, often those who are comfortable speaking in groups, while increasing the participation of those who are less likely to share their opinions, often considered to be introverts. To maximize one's influence as a leader, one must first maximize access to information and important data. Creating conditions that encourage people to push past boundaries of power and perceived importance is critical. One of the most important places for educational leaders to acknowledge and address power differentials is during school meetings.

School Meetings and Assumptions

Meetings occur often in schools; perhaps too often. Each one presents an opportunity to experience the culture of the school and learn how things operate. Just as meetings can help educational leaders understand the sense of belonging their teachers and staff experience, they also teach a great deal about communication practices. We depend on conversations with teachers to better understand the culture of schools. Following are some of the questions we ask to help us understand their experiences in meetings:

- ◆ How do meetings typically work at your school?
- ◆ Is there a common structure for meetings?
- ◆ When you use agendas for meetings, how are they developed and by whom?
- ◆ Are you able to participate in meetings as much as you would like? If not, what is preventing you from speaking up?
- ◆ Do you leave meetings feeling like your voice is valued?
- ◆ Do you have a chance to talk about your ideas, ask questions, and share your authentic perspective at meetings?

Educator responses to these questions vary considerably from one school to the next. That being said, since requests for consultation typically come from schools looking to change their school culture and improve their communication practices, several themes consistently emerge. First, educators typically report that their experiences at meetings are generally unsatisfactory. The organizational structures of meetings are controlled by one or two team members, and others are rarely given opportunities to provide suggestions. Teachers also report meetings feel overly rigid and follow the same patterns regardless of the topic being discussed or problem to be solved. Those in authority typically talk the most, and people with opposing viewpoints rarely speak up during the meeting—although they have plenty to say afterwards.

Often at meetings, educators feel decisions were made before they got there. This contributes to the reluctance of teachers to speak up when they do not agree with the group or the direction of the conversation. Teachers participating in meetings like this will develop an external locus of control at work, believing events and decisions made at the school are only influenced by factors outside of their control. In contrast, individuals with an internal locus of control believe, or have learned, that they can influence outcomes based on the decisions they make or the contributions they offer at meetings.

Educators also report discussions from school meetings or decisions made there do not consistently impact school or teacher practices. Long discussions and brainstorming sessions take place, generating numerous potential solutions. Once the meeting ends and everyone returns to the frantic pace of their jobs, follow-through often is lacking. When the team reconvenes, inconsistent efforts to implement an action plan make it difficult to determine if the unsuccessful intervention was due to the plan itself or its execution.

These perceptions about meetings provide a springboard to experiment with new approaches and strategies to improve the value of meetings for participants and, most importantly, to create conditions allowing for the transfer of important data and information among educators and their leaders. First and foremost, it is important to establish sets of assumptions aimed at guiding conversations through difficult periods. Making explicit assumptions of how we expect and believe communication should occur improve the chances open and honest dialogue will take place. Naming these assumptions helps sets a foundation and target goal. Consider the following assumptions derived from the work of Roger Schwarz (2016, p. 61).

◆ I have information; so do other people.
◆ Each of us sees things others don't.
◆ People may disagree with me and still have pure motives.
◆ Differences are opportunities for learning.
◆ How might I be contributing to the problem?

The first four assumptions explicitly set forth foundation for conversation. No one has access to all information. Each of us has a unique vantage point from which we see the world. The third assumption focuses on not second-guessing people's intentions when their views are different from our own. The fourth assumption asserts differences are opportunities for learning rather than painful disruptions to the comfort level of the team. The final statement, posed as a question, is founded on the assumption we almost always contribute to a problem in ways that might not be visible at first.

Sometimes we contribute to a problem by being silent (i.e., choosing to not speak up or raise an issue with those who would benefit greatly from hearing it). It is critical for school leaders to share their concerns regarding the power of silence, and to foster school cultures that reduce the likelihood of educators withholding their ideas, opinions, or concerns; all of which provides valuable data to inform decision-making, but only if they are shared with the group responsible for change. When educators begin the process of examining complex problems, such as weak participation by certain subgroups in honors courses, they often begin their analysis by examining factors and causes that lie outside themselves (e.g., prior school experiences, parenting, or perhaps weak leadership). While those factors clearly warrant consideration and discussion, it is critical that the examination not end there, leaving our contributions out of the equation.

These assumptions seem sensible. Still, we cannot emphasize enough how uncommon they are with the teams and groups with whom we work across the country. What we more typically find as we observe behaviors in groups are assumptions/norms that approach what Roger Schwarz

(p. 41) describes as a more "unilateral" approach. Here are some of the beliefs that characterize a unilateral approach to group dynamics:

+ I am right; those who disagree with me are wrong.
+ I understand the situation; those who disagree with me, don't.
+ I am not contributing to the problem.
+ I have pure motives; those who disagree with me have questionable motives.

You rarely see these assumptions written down. Nevertheless, these unspoken assumptions influence group dynamics and are reinforced by repeated exchanges between leaders and those who disagree with them. Team members may experience meetings guided by these assumptions as normal or even acceptable because they are so common. Sadly, these dynamics will limit the flow of information, prevent people from addressing important issues openly and honestly, and block access to critical data.

Naming the assumptions providing tacit parameters for school meetings is only half the battle. Targets often are not reached. It is essential to assess how enmeshed these assumptions are at each of our meetings. One key indicator is how often educational leaders are able to engage and capture the multiple perspectives present at meetings.

Accepting Multiple Perspectives

One key step in moving from a unilateral framework to a culture of mutual learning occurs when we shift our mindset from somebody is right or wrong to the idea there are multiple perspectives to be examined. If we get stuck in the "one of us is right, and it is probably me" rut, it is difficult to make progress on challenging issues. Difficult issues are complex because there are multiple factors influencing situations. Our conversational goal, like the alternative ping-pong game, must move from winning an argument to understanding how others think about an issue. One of the reasons our current political climate is so tense is because there is a "you are either with me or against me" mentality. Ensuring participants understand the importance of this shift in the conversation is critical.

It takes practice and skill to become curious in the face of ideas or perspectives that sound, at first, nonsensical. To be authentically curious about the rationale behind someone's point of view and able to share with the speaker an effective summary of the main idea, as well as the feelings behind the perspective, is the first step in creating a dialogue. We call this "listening in stereo." When an educational leader is able to capture and summarize the concerns of a group member, they will often receive an acknowledgment from the speaker like "I could not have said it better myself." The leader is then well-positioned to respond with something like "Well, I have a different perspective." Usually, the original speaker ex-presses some kind of interest at that moment to find out more, which begins an authentic dialogue driven by understanding and a mutual commitment to problem-solving. With this as your fuel, educators are in a much better position to make informed decisions that consider the multiple perspectives present in the group.

Avoiding Groupthink

Gilovich and Ross (2015) discuss the perils of groupthink using the common example of leaders starting a meeting by asking each member of the group to share their thoughts about a problem. While this approach sounds promising, the results are typically disappointing. "Rather than leading to a free flow of ideas, the range of possibilities under discussion quickly narrows. Two processes limit the diversity of opinions, one deliberate and the other unintentional" (p. 155). These two processes, self-censorship and the common knowledge effect, are both associated with the literature pertaining to groupthink, which was first identified more than 50 years ago and has been subsequently researched by social psychologists since that time. The term "groupthink" was coined by Irving Janis in 1972, who defined it as "a kind of thinking in which maintaining group cohesiveness and solidarity is more important than considering the facts in a realistic manner" (Aronson, Wilson, & Akert, 2010, p. 267).

The first symptom of groupthink is self-censorship, which sets in when group members feel pressure to agree with the majority opinion. This is consistent with normative social influence (Chapter 4). Just as participants in the Asch line experiment choose the wrong response despite knowing the correct answer, group members offer support for positions other than their own when the stakes are high and pressure for consensus is unstated but powerful. To avoid self-censorship, educational leaders should ask group members to share their perspectives privately, perhaps by writing them down and submitting them to one group member who, in turn, shares them anonymously with everyone—inviting responses and conversation. Another option would be to break up the group into smaller groups for brainstorming sessions, which are then reported to the larger group for discussion.

Gilovich and Ross also refer to the "common knowledge effect," or a failure to share unique information. When group members are brought together to better understand and ultimately solve a problem, the common knowledge effect results in the group spending a majority of their time discussing things already known by all members (i.e., common knowledge) rather than inviting members to share unique knowledge relevant to the problem. As a result, group discussions are unnecessarily shallow and limited in scope, which directly impedes their ability to solve problems. Group members with certain expertise might not share their knowledge, which could be critical to solving the problem at hand.

The common knowledge effect was evident when observing a special education team deliberating their use of retention for elementary students struggling in reading. The group appeared to agree retention should be rare, but repeating earlier grades (i.e., kindergarten through second grade) would expose children to additional reading support and reduce the demands being placed on special education teachers to help them "catch up." When one group member shared the overwhelming majority of research on retention was negative and did not support its practice for students struggling with reading, other group members quickly dismissed the comment and responded with personal narratives regarding the benefits of retention for family members or former students. The response silenced the concerned team member, and the conversation ended with a tacit agreement to continue the current retention practices.

In a follow-up conversation with the principal at that school, we shared our impressions from the meeting and brought up the exchange regarding retention. We shared that one member of his team appeared to have important knowledge, perhaps even expertise, that others should take the time to consider prior to making any final decisions about the use of retention at the school. The principal agreed and eventually asked the team member to prepare a short presentation for the group and share any resources related to retention others could read in advance of the meeting. Not only did this empower and validate that team member, we later learned it helped create a strong sense of belonging for him, as well. The presentation and sharing of resources in advance allowed the team to expand their shared knowledge, which ultimately led to the school's commitment to no longer recommend students for retention.

Establishing a culture that encourages and values open and honest communication allows school leaders to fully understand the challenges and problems present in their buildings and districts. It communicates to educators that their experiences, beliefs, and values are important and will be considered by others who are hoping to create a school environment where everyone can thrive. The success of a school, however, is rarely a linear progression. Educators must be challenged to learn from both their successes and failures, which is why *Encouraging Experimentation* is the fourth and final condition for change in our framework.

References

Aronson, E., Wilson, T. D., & Akert, R. M. (2010). *Social psychology* (7th ed.). Pearson.

Barth, R. (2002). The culture builder. *Education Leadership, 59*(8), 6–11.

Edmondson, A. C. (2019). *The fearless organization: Creating psychological safety in the workplace for learning, innovation, and growth.* Wiley and Sons.

Gilovich, T., & Ross, L. (2015). *The wisest one in the room: How you can benefit from social psychology's most powerful insights.* Free Press.

Saphier, J., & King, M. (1985). Good seeds grow in strong cultures. *Educational Leadership, 42*(6), 67–74.

Schwarz, R. M. (2016). *The skilled facilitator: A comprehensive resource for consultants, facilitators, coaches, and trainers* (3rd ed.). Jossey-Bass.

6

Encouraging Experimentation

Introduction

The purpose of this chapter and inclusion of *Encouraging Experimentation* as one of the four conditions of our framework is to help school leaders understand and appreciate the importance of having educators view their work as a series of experiments designed to help them improve over time. Educators are "scientists of learning," and, as such, they need to act like scientists, developing and assessing lessons like mini-experiments with the hope of making discoveries and maximizing student achievement. Consider the following reflection from a veteran teacher we consulted as an example of a developing scientist of learning.

A Scientist of Learning—Math Instruction

This is my 10th year as a 7th grade math teacher, and in some ways, it feels like my first. My practice goal from my educator evaluation plan this year was to learn more about the emotional underpinnings of student attitudes towards learning math. While I have a strong content knowledge base and a decent tool kit of teaching strategies, I have struggled to effectively accommodate students with anxiety and poor academic self-confidence. I decided in the fall to take a deep dive into this arena.

I started by reading *Emotional Intelligence* (Goleman, 2005) and *Mindset* (Dweck, 2006), books that had become quite popular in my district. Many colleagues had read them as part of their PLCs. Both were eye openers. I learned from Goleman how much feelings influence one's openness to learning. From Dweck, I gained deeper understanding of how adult feedback to students after they are successful at something can influence their ability to persevere in the face of setbacks. I was eager to apply these new lessons about student learning in my classroom.

My student learning goal focused on the lowest three students in each of my five classes. I conducted some screenings to collect information about their understanding of fractions, decimals, and percentages, as well as their attitudes towards math. My stretch goal was to demonstrate growth in both domains based on an attitudinal survey I administered at the beginning and end of the school year, as well as skill assessments I conducted three times during the school year. Part of my work towards both goals involved meeting with a guidance counselor, a special educator, and a school psychologist, all of whom were working with my small group of students in different capacities. Their insights, like the books I read, broadened my understanding of the students' social emotional needs and how they related to achievement in math.

The counselor and school psychologist helped me understand how "little" things, like greeting the students at the door and learning about their interests, could strengthen my relationships with them and increase their willingness to persevere when lessons became challenging. My special education colleague helped me understand the importance of soliciting feedback from my students on a daily basis. She suggested I ask each student to rate the challenge level associated with my learning goals for the day, as well as the level of effort they had applied to the assignment—both on a simple 1–5 scale. Collecting this information from my students not only informed my instruction, but it also raised student awareness of the importance of effort and its relationship with achievement.

I wish I could tell you this resulted in all 15 of my students meeting grade-level expectations for math and developing a new love for the subject. I am a bit embarrassed to say on a pure skill level, only six of my students showed significant improvement, while seven stayed the same and two of the student's achievement scores actually decreased. Fortunately, the survey data indicated all of the students' feelings towards math were more positive at the end of the school year. While I think their improved attitude towards math is an encouraging outcome, it is clearly not sufficient without an accompanying increase in achievement. I am frustrated that my efforts did not lead to more skill development.

My initial analysis of the problem led me to believe many of my students lacked the basic math skills I consider to be prerequisite knowledge for my classes, and my interventions did not address those gaps in a deep enough way. Students who did show progress did not present with these significant gaps, or they were small enough I was able to catch them up sufficiently so they could access the lessons I presented. I am not sure how I can build that bridge for students when the gaps are more substantial in the future, but I am placing my bets technology will play a role in the solution. I think if I can use an innovative software program to provide personalized work for students who are lacking some of the prerequisite skills for my classes, I might see better results.

I also think that for the two students whose scores diminished, their inconsistent progress may be related to memory deficits rather than skill deficits. They struggle with remembering the previous day's lesson, despite showing some insight and ability at the moment. I am not sure how to address this issue because I am not an expert on learning problems due to memory difficulties, but this will be a place I want to expand my practice in the upcoming year. Looking ahead, I would like to construct a practice goal that expands my toolkit to include strategies for working with students with memory issues. I also plan to do a deep dive into what particular technology programs in math could amplify my ability to address the more significant prerequisite "missing" skills that are part of my students' profiles.

When we present this reflection to seasoned educational administrators, we hear a range of reactions that reflect a number of the points we discuss in this chapter. The reflection engenders rich conversations about the role data collection plays in the development of successful teaching practices. The current educational climate has little tolerance for less than optimal results. The honest, deep thinking this teacher expresses, in combination with her willingness to try new approaches, positions her well for continuous improvement in service of her students. Despite her missed goals, the thinking and reflection embedded in this vignette represent the qualities we think are critical and will ultimately spur forward progress. The following sections provide additional support for the importance of encouraging experimentation and prioritizing continuous improvement in schools.

Growth Mindset

Encouraging experimentation is based on the belief that improvement is an iterative process based on evaluation and effort. In education, this means the growth and evolution of educational leaders and teachers depend on their ability to continuously evaluate the results of their work and persist when times become challenging. Notably, the focus on improvement makes it clear that constructs such as intelligence, creativity, flexibility, and organization should not be considered fixed. This lies at the heart of Dr. Carol Dweck's best-selling book *Mindset* (2006), in which she describes two primary types of mindset that have long-lasting implications for the way people live their lives. Dweck defines those with fixed mindsets as "believing that your qualities are carved in stone" (p. 6). In contrast, she states a growth mindset "is based on the belief that your basic qualities are things you can cultivate through your effort" (p. 7). Since encouraging experimentation in the interest of improvement is one of our framework's conditions for change, we believe a growth mindset is essential for educators.

Dweck's research indicates when individuals with a growth mindset experience challenges or setbacks in life, they do not respond by pulling back from the learning challenge, blaming themselves, or questioning the expectation or demand. Instead, they become curious as to *how* they might solve the problem, rather than wondering *if* they can solve the problem. Similarly, a growth mindset leads one to view mistakes as part of learning and not a sign of weakness. While we have witnessed a significant increase in schools that have applied Dweck's research about the benefits of cultivating a growth mindset with students, we have observed inconsistent application of this important work with regards to the interactions between the four perspectives from our framework.

For example, when a growth mindset is present, we have consultation meetings with school-based teams that begin with comments like, "We haven't quite figured out how to integrate our behavioral program into the larger school, which is resulting in frustrated teachers and isolated students." During a conversation with an experienced superintendent, we heard the following, "I'm really struggling to connect with new school committee members. Our meetings have included consistent stalemates and accusations that do not feel fair, which has resulted in several unproductive meetings." Finally, a parent shared the following when asked about her child's experience at the school, "My son had a great year in kindergarten. He connected right away with the teacher and seemed to be friends with all of his classmates. This year has been a little different. He and his teacher don't appear to be a great match yet, but I can tell it's getting better. He still seems to have a lot of friends, so I'm hopeful we will get back to where we were by the end of the year."

Based on how the problems were framed and presented to us in each of these cases, we were encouraged because it was clear the team possessed a growth mindset. Had there been a fixed mindset, the school-based team might have reported, "Our behavioral program stinks. The kids are completely out of control, and the teachers only make things worse. They don't even like the kids." A superintendent with a fixed mindset may have sought support by reporting, "The new members of the school committee are total jerks and have no idea how schools work. We have not had one productive meeting since they

joined the committee. I don't know how they can't see that!"
And with a fixed mindset, the parent may have complained,
"First grade is a lost cause. The teacher makes no effort to
connect with the kids. I wish my son could have looped with his
kindergarten teacher. She was the best!" A fixed mindset would
have made our job far more challenging.

When working with school-based teams or educators with a
fixed mindset, the options for problem-solving are limited because they do not recognize potential for growth or change in
the people involved. If parents decide a teacher is not a good
match for their son, the only plausible solutions include changing the teacher or moving the student—both of which are
usually nonstarters for elementary principals. The first step
when consulting school leaders or school-based teams with a
fixed mindset is to identify it as a major obstacle to making
progress. For example, we have said, "It sounds like you're not
happy with the current status of your behavior program, and
both your teachers and students are having a difficult time. In
our experience, these programs are among the toughest to get
right for elementary schools. Let's start by seeing if we can
identify anything that appears to be working about the program
and then discuss options for improvement."

Encouraging a growth mindset in educators is an important
factor in developing a culture that embraces innovation and
continuous improvement. Principals and other leaders can influence the mindset of educators by observing their successes
carefully and providing feedback that specifically names the
strategies and approaches they used to achieve that success.
This parallel between work with students and professional development between educational leaders and staff members is
linked to the fractal nature of schools (Ash & D'Auria, 2012). A
fractal is a geometric figure, each part of which has the same
statistical character as the whole (Merriam-Webster, 2020). The
fractal nature of schools, therefore, suggests the relationships
that are conducive to learning and improvement are the same
between the four groups of stakeholders within our framework.
Superintendents should be supportive and curious as they work
with their principals in the same way teachers should work with

students. This theme relies on members of the community viewing problems and challenges with a growth mindset.

Improvement Science

Directly connected to Dweck's research on mindsets, numerous initiatives from the Carnegie Foundation for the Improvement of Teaching have emerged within a newly-formed area called *improvement science*. Its chief architect, Anthony Bryk, suggests improvement science is a disciplined approach to altering educational practices in order to benefit students. In their book *Learning to Improve: How American Schools Can Get Better at Getting Better* (2015), Bryk et al. suggest educators need to learn from other industries and focus on improving systems rather than critiquing or praising individuals. Consider the following passage from the book:

> The quality chasm in medicine is instructive for educa-tors. As noted previously, medicine benefits from great science, it invests heavily in developing its people, and it supports them with extraordinary technology that en-hances their efficacy. Not surprisingly, educational reformers see all three of these factors as critical to improving the U.S. educational system. And they are right; we do need a stronger knowledge base, better professional education programs, and more effective use of technology to advance student learning. Yet, as in medicine, developments along any one of these lines alone is not likely to redress the unsatisfactory student outcomes we now see. And, they may even increase inequities in the years ahead (p. 60).

The implications are overwhelming. Bryk et al. go on to discuss several national education initiatives that have failed to produce sustainable and repeatable change, including when the Gates Foundation invested $2 billion to restructure high schools to create smaller learning environments only to discontinue the initiative and withdraw funding seven years later, shifting their focus to eliminating bad teachers, identifying good ones, and raising salaries to draw stronger candidates into the teaching profession and prevent them from leaving.

Improvement science researchers use examples like this to explain the importance of experiments and using reliable and valid data to determine which interventions work and to what extent they can be generalized to other school environments. By taking the time to diagnose the problem accurately, professionals from all industries can avoid what Bryk et al., refer to as *solutionitis*, or "the propensity to jump quickly on a solution before fully understanding the exact problem to be solved" (p. 24). As with the Gates Foundation story, we find the following helpful when talking with school-based teams about the importance of experiments and core ideas from improvement science.

Prior to starting a workshop with a group of educators, the authors heard a story on National Public Radio (NPR) about a failed experimental trial for a new drug that had promise as a cure for a certain type of cancer. We shared a synopsis of the news story to the participants and asked, "As a result of this failed experiment, what do you think happened to the scientists involved?" Some popular responses from the room full of educators included: "The scientists got fired," "The scientists lost their jobs," or "Nothing happened." In reality, the scientists published a paper in a journal because their failed experiment produced results helpful to the field. The failed experiment produced insights into what did not work and potentially new approaches that could address the limitations encountered in this study.

Despite years of research and experimentation, medical science has not found a cure for cancer. Progress unquestionably has been made, but along the way there have been failures and hopeful pathways that became dead ends. In education, we have not yet figured out how to close achievement gaps that have roots in poverty, homelessness, learning disabilities, and racism. Progress has been made in some areas, but experimentation needs to continue. Part of that work will involve learning from errors and setbacks. What educational leaders do with knowledge gained from failed initiatives is equally important. Consider a second powerful quote from Bryk, Gomez, Grunow, and LeMahieu (2015).

> When we see unsatisfactory results, we tend to blame the individuals most immediately connected to those results, not recognizing the full causes. The evidence from over a half century of effort across numerous sectors and industries is clear: improving productivity in complex systems is not principally about incentivizing more individual effort, preaching about better intentions, or even enhancing individual competence. Rather, it is about designing better processes for carrying out common work problems and creating more agile mechanisms for sensing and reacting to novel situations. In high-performing organizations, failures are seen not principally as a reason to cast blame, but as occasions to learn. Data are not blunt instruments for imposing sanctions and offering rewards; they are resources used to deepen understanding of current operations and to generate insights about where to focus efforts to improve (p. 61).

This perfectly captures the valuable contributions of improvement science for educational leaders, which greatly influenced the development of our framework.

Experiments in Education

For some educators, the combination of experimentation and children sounds scary and uncomfortable. While we understand these emotions, we also realize embracing improvement will require adult learning. One way we have attempted to reframe how educators think about these concepts is by describing the assumptions underlying teaching. When teachers construct lesson plans, they are, for all intents and purposes, designing an experiment. There is no guarantee the experiment will be successful with all students. In fact, that is rarely the case. More likely it is that some of the students will achieve all of the objectives, some will achieve a few of the objectives, and still others might not—for a wide variety of reasons—achieve any. Our experiences in schools suggest this is normally what occurs in classrooms every day.

Educational researcher John Hattie suggests one of the most important aspects of effective teaching is assessing one's impact. Who are the students who fall into each category above? Knowing one's impact is, in effect, being a scientist of learning. Our lesson plans are experiments. We never know for certain if our "experiments" work with all students. In fact, it is not unusual for secondary teachers to note a lesson plan worked quite well with one class but was less effective with another.

Variables impacting student learning are multitudinous. A rough night of sleep, a fight on the playground, not eating breakfast, or a comment made in the hallway can easily impact a student's readiness to learn. What we find more concerning, however, is the hidden assumption that if one is an effective teacher, then all their students will achieve all learning objectives all the time. This assumption is unrealistic. It also makes trying new strategies more risky than necessary. If educators start with an assumption that 100% of their students should be successful when they deploy their traditional approaches to a lesson, then learning new approaches and incorporating them into their repertoire feels untenable. Teachers need to know that they will not be successful right away with all students. Students will struggle to connect with the lessons at times, and some may even fail to grasp the concepts that are being introduced, even though many of their classmates are achieving mastery. Instead of striving for perfection, teachers must reset their expectations and plan to learn from both their successful and unsuccessful instructional approaches. If teachers assume that traditional approaches should be 100% effective, then the gap between their expectations and reality will feel like an insurmountable separation.

Establishing conditions that will tolerate "small experiments" and the requisite analysis of those experiments (i.e., what worked, what didn't, and why) should be the ultimate priority for educational leaders, as this is the heart and soul of effective teaching and essential for those engaging in continuous improvement. Some educators have shared they understand this framework, but when they figure out after a lesson who achieved the objectives and who did not, they wonder what is expected if, on their own, they cannot figure out what is needed to address the variance in the class' learning. If we harken back to Edmondson's research, "not knowing" and "asking for help" are two skills demonstrated by people in learning organizations. Collaboration with students, parents, special educators, school psychologists, fellow teachers, and instructional coaches are all possibilities for addressing the "What do I do next?" question. This kind of collaboration, however, will only work well if people believe asking for help is not a sign of weakness but is actually what effective teachers do when faced with complex instructional issues.

The aspects of our framework are interconnected. Without sufficient psychological safety, experimentation and learning from mistakes will not occur consistently. Without trust derived from a sense of belonging, educators will be reluctant to ask for assistance when stuck or raise questions when they need more clarity. When people are not involved in problem diagnosis, they will not be committed to the solutions that emanate from study of the problem. Consistent improvement occurs when conditions are ripe for honesty, safety, trust, collaboration, and experimentation. Our framework represents important puzzle pieces to the complex issues that often keep schools stuck in how educators used to do things, rather than how we might do things to better serve the needs of students.

References

Ash, P. B., & D'Auria, J. P. (2012). *School systems that learn: Improving professional practice, overcoming limitations, and diffusing innovation* (1st ed.). Corwin.

Bryk, A. S., Gomez, L. M., Grunow, A., & LeMahieu, P. G. (2015). *Learning to improve: How America's schools can get better and getting better.* Harvard Education Press.

Dweck, C. S. (2006). *Mindset: How you can fulfil your potential*. Random House.

Fractal. (2020). *Merriam-Webster*. Retrieved from https://www.merriam-webster.com/dictionary/fractal.

Goleman, D. (2005). *Emotional intelligence: Why it can matter more than IQ* (10th Anniversary ed.). Bantam.

PART III

Applying the Framework

7

A Leadership Guide—Moving from Theory to Practice

Introduction

Part I focuses on improving the vision of educational leaders. We attempt to illuminate how leaders can improve their vision in the face of challenging situations or problems by examining different perspectives and dimensions of an issue. Part II discusses the four conditions for change essential for school communities to thrive. Conditions for change ensure educators share their successes and failures to both promote promising practices and learn from mistakes. Open and honest communication practices and widespread feelings of belonging create a sense of commitment that fosters collaboration and maximizes opportunities for learning and improvement. Balance between psychological safety and accountability promotes innovation and risk-taking, while prioritizing constructive feedback and improvement. These four key conditions raise the probability that any strategies emerging from "improved vision" lead to sustainable improvement and progress. A visual representation of our framework is shown in Figure 7.1.

The following infographic visually depicts our framework including the four distinct perspectives critical to improving

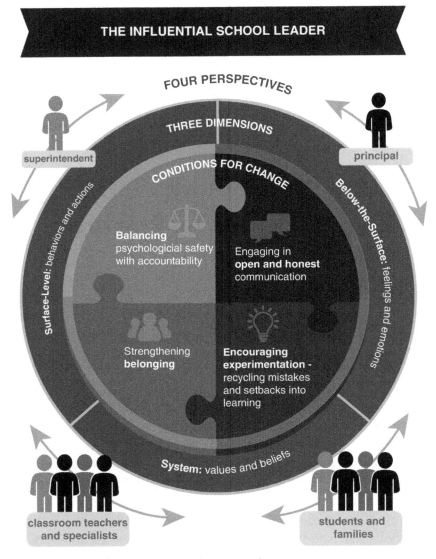

FIGURE 7.1 The Influential School Leader Framework

vision, the three dimensions of a problem, and the critical conditions for change that allow teams to authentically examine root causes of problems and develop strategies to address them. To gain confidence in applying the framework, Table 7.1 offers a

Step	Objective	Description
1	Establish a small but diverse committee of stakeholders.	◆ Include 10–12 participants. ◆ Include representatives from each stakeholder group. ◆ Diversity is critical.
2	Share the assumptions and structures that will guide the group's conversations.	◆ Expect multiple perspectives. ◆ Disagreements are critical to learning. ◆ Listen for the quiet voice. ◆ Use an exit survey to capture information that went unstated.
3	Develop a shared understanding of the problem BEFORE diving into further discussions.	◆ Clearly define the problem to foster inner acceptance for members of the group. ◆ Hold small group discussions to give everyone an opportunity to contribute. ◆ Write down the shared understanding for the group to review.
4	Verify that the problem statement reflects the group's understanding and concerns.	◆ Seek input and agreement that the team captured the problem accurately. ◆ Emphasize the importance of a comprehensive understanding of the problem. ◆ Invite disagreement and acknowledge the importance of diverse perspectives.
5	Start an inquiry conversation to uncover what external factors are contributing to the problem.	◆ Emphasize each perspective is contributing to the problem in its own way. ◆ Make an effort to avoid blame. ◆ Acknowledge feelings but do not avoid them.
6	After reviewing external factors, switch the focus to internal factors. "How might I be contributing to the problem?"	◆ The facilitator/leader needs to raise this question explicitly with the group. ◆ It will not be surprising, however, if the group responds initially with silence. ◆ This is a challenging question that tests the psychological safety of the group as well as each individual's capacity to be vulnerable.
7	Integrate the external factors with the internal factors to provide a map of the contribution system.	◆ This shapes a graphic organizer that helps participants visualize the forces contributing to the problem. ◆ Share the map of the contribution system with the larger faculty and request feedback.

(Cont.)

Step	Objective	Description
		◆ The group should discuss relationships within aspects of the contribution system.
		◆ Identify targets for intervention within the system.
8	Brainstorm possible "small experiments" that might address factors contributing to the problem/challenge.	◆ Track the outcomes of these experiments.
		◆ Create a way to document what people learn from their experiments.
		◆ Make sure the lessons learned from the experiments are used to inform decisions and interventions moving forward.
9	A decision-making process should be discussed and communicated to the team in advance of any decisions that impact staff.	◆ Use the results of small experiments to establish school-wide approaches.
		◆ Identify processes for selecting strategies that will be recommended/required for staff to use in their work with students.
		◆ Identify decision-makers for the group.

TABLE 7.1   Influential School Leader—Guidelines (Cont.)

sequence of nine steps, with corresponding objectives, that educational leaders can use to implement the framework.

Step 1: Establish a Small, Diverse Committee

Eight members is an optimal size for the committee, as it allows two representatives from each of the four perspectives. Although workable groups can expand to as many as 12 people, as the size of a group increases, the time each member contributes to discussions diminishes. While educational leaders are reluctant to deny interested teachers or staff members opportunities to participate, it is important to remind members of the school community that small, diverse committees work best and group participants will change regularly. Most will have opportunities to serve during the school year.

It is essential to prioritize diversity. Failure to do so

diminishes the group's impact, as well as the commitment needed to implement strategies or approaches from the group. When tackling an issue where staff is divided, be sure each viewpoint is represented equally within the group. Diversity should also include people who play different roles within the relevant system. In a school setting, that means including members of various departments and grade levels, as well as people representing the four perspectives from the framework. Although the size and scope of the problem will dictate whether or not specific members of the school community should be involved, such as the superintendent or the students, including diverse perspectives should always be a priority. Ensuring diversity related to both gender and race also is important. This can be a challenge in elementary schools at times, as a majority of teachers tend to be female, but there are myriad factors that can help diversify the membership of the small group.

Leaders looking to improve their vision must seek out a diversity of perspectives and lean into the discomfort of disagreements that will inevitably emerge from those differences. This dynamic will only be possible if the people at the table have different views.

Step 2: Share Assumptions and Structures

Assumptions and norms help set expectations and create a sense of safety and belonging. While participants may act in ways that violate the group norms, establishing them at the onset allows participants to address out-of-sync behaviors. While not an easy task, it is more effective to discuss behaviors before challenges or conflicts arise. When discussed following a violation of the assumptions, the ensuing conversations often become personal, attributing negative behaviors to the personalities of participants, resulting in defensiveness and making change unlikely.

We often recommend using the assumptions articulated by Schwarz (2016):

1. I have information; so do other people.
2. Each of us sees things that others don't.
3. People may disagree with me and still have pure motives.
4. Differences are opportunities for learning.
5. How might I be contributing to the problem?

These assumptions encourage the sharing of information at the heart of improving our vision. Answering "How might I be contributing to the problem?" can surprise participants. People enter groups with assumptions they are seeking to solve problems existing independently of them. Asking group members to reflect on this question means they will have to examine their own behaviors and emotions in addition to external factors contributing to the problem. Participants must be introduced to the possibility there might be ways they contribute to the problem. When discussed at the group's orientation, it is helpful to point out that one can contribute to the problem by remaining silent (e.g., the NASA engineer from Chapter 5). Educators sometimes contribute to a problem when they are aware of issues but are uncomfortable discussing them or bringing them to the attention of those who need to hear them most. Introducing the idea that one's silence can be a contributing factor that helps others resonate with this assumption.

This group orientation is a good time to explain key organizational practices that will be part of the group process. One practice we strongly recommend is providing an anonymous electronic survey at the end of each meeting. The results should be presented to the group at the next meeting. This technique provides participants a way to provide feedback to group facilitators about how the group is functioning, the degree to which people are acting in accordance with the assumptions, and an opportunity to raise issues they might not feel sharing with the group face to face.

Step 3: Develop a Shared Understanding

It is helpful to begin the group's work by asking people to define the problem. As you hear people's thoughts, create a document showing the development of a problem statement. People think writing a problem statement is easy and obvious. It is not, as group members often have different initial perspectives on how to describe the problem at hand. This is an opportunity to link the assumptions to the work of the group (e.g., each of us sees things others do not). As group members begin to understand that others view the problem differently, their understanding of the problem shifts.

For example, while working with a leadership team trying to address the challenge of reopening schools after months of online learning during summer 2020, a group began to see through discussions that teachers were not only fearful of getting sick but also worried about how to manage a range of new issues and technologies. Fear of incompetence emerged as an important aspect of how teachers were feeling as they approached reopening the school. Had that not surfaced, the team would not have understood this was a critical challenge they were facing. Without identifying this factor, it would have been impossible to develop strategies to offset it. Fortunately, the teacher's fear of incompetence was identified by the group and incorporated into the school reopening plan.

Step 4: Verify the Problem Statement

Once the team captures the important contours of the problem, it should seek input from the full faculty to test whether the team has captured it accurately. At this point, the group has not discussed causes of the problem. The work has focused solely on developing a shared description of the problem. The full faculty often will spot missed or underestimated aspects of the problem in the description. This check-in enhances the commitment of faculty to the process and, ultimately, to the strategies they will be asked to deploy. Such commitment is as important as the understanding that emerges from this process. Implementation of strategies is ineffective without commitment from the staff.

Step 5: Inquiry Conversation—Considering External Factors

With a problem statement in hand, it is time to uncover external factors contributing to the problem (as defined in Step 3). Often during the initial aspect of this inquiry cycle, participants will look outside of themselves. It is not unusual for people to blame those outside of their perspective. Teachers sometimes blame parents or the principal. Principals sometimes blame the central office or teachers. When this happens, the group can get stuck in a rut, leaving people feeling frustrated and resentful. Additionally, people getting blamed often feel defensive and angry. Defensiveness damages the group's understanding of the problem. This is a critical time to acknowledge feelings and become curious about other perspectives. If a principal, for example, is being blamed, it can be helpful if he or she can become curious about what others are saying and restate what is heard rather than becoming defensive. Understanding what others are saying is different from agreeing with their point of view. In order to offer a different perspective, one must first understand the perspective of others. Understanding precedes agreement or disagreement.

Step 6: "How Might I Be Contributing to the Problem?"

After reviewing external factors, ask each member to answer the following question: "How might I be contributing to the problem?" The facilitator must raise this question explicitly with the group. It is a critical moment for the team. The group may respond to this challenging question with silence, as it tests the psychological safety of the group, as well as each individual's capacity to be vulnerable. Do not attempt to "fill the silence." The facilitator may say, "I don't know how to interpret your silence." Groups able to address their own contributions have a much better chance of moving past mediocrity and achieving excellence. Facilitators must be patient. It can be scary to cross this threshold. An anonymous survey at the end of each meeting provides an opportunity for people reluctant to share their ideas during meetings to provide responses afterward.

Step 7: Map the Contribution System

The original problem often transforms as honest insights and discussions reveal different aspects and layers previously unseen. When the team combines external and internal factors, a detailed map of the forces and factors contributing to the problem emerges. A new way of understanding the problem arising from the group's collective insights is both exciting and energizing. It literally can feel like an *Aha!* or discovery moment.

This is an opportune time to once again check in with the larger faculty to share how the group's understanding of the problem has shifted and seek their input and reactions. This check-in keeps faculty informed and involved in the process. Involvement results in a willingness to commit to the outcomes of the process.

Step 8: Brainstorm Possible "Small Experiments"

Now begins an experimental phase where strategies are created to address the underlying issues uncovered by the team. Brainstorming possible "small experiments" addressing contributing factors to the problem/challenge allows educators to discover possible solutions or ways to ameliorate the issue. Experiments should seek to test possible mitigating ways to address factors that have been hypothesized. Starting "small" means trying new approaches with one class for a short period of time, multiple classes for a few days, or with a subset of students. Small experiments provide insight and understanding.

It is critical to create ways to collect and gather what is learned from the experiments. More than whether they worked or not, it is vital educators learn from both failures and successes. Educators become scientists of learning, which represents a significant shift in school culture. Educators slowly gain experience in creating inquiry cycles investigating approaches and collecting data. When schools started to "experiment" with online learning in spring 2020, not all approaches were equally successful or effective. Many schools did not consider how data could help them ascertain which approaches to online learning were most effective. Consequently, as schools began to consider online learning for fall 2020, they did not have access to insights gained from a more structured approach to the online platform "experiment." Keeping track of "small experiments" helps build a knowledge base all educators can access.

Step 9: Establish a Decision-Making Process

Strategies that appear to work should be considered as possible school-wide approaches. How will the decision be made to select a strategy and recommend/require all staff to use it with students? Will the principal make the decision? Will the team make the decision? Will the full faculty decide? It is critical that team members understand how decisions will be made. Leaders must communicate the decision-making process to the larger group (the faculty) in advance of any decisions impacting staff. While various approaches to decision making have an array of both benefits and drawbacks, educators generally will support decisions when they had involvement in the process and understand in advance how final decisions are made.

An unintentional benefit at this point is that the team assembled to study the problem and make recommendations often transitions into a leadership team. These nine steps provide a professional development opportunity where team members learn to study and analyze complex issues, learn how to disagree and challenge one another's ideas without damaging relationships, and develop approaches and strategies to complex issues that are owned by the faculty. The process can be repeated to study and develop new approaches to any challenge schools need to address. Through practice, educational leaders can become scientists of learning.

Reference

Schwarz, R. M. (2016). *The skilled facilitator: A comprehensive resource for consultants, facilitators, coaches, and trainers* (3rd ed.). Jossey-Bass.

8

Preparing for Change

Introduction

Providing a structure for the application of our framework in schools is a necessary step towards changing the culture and the processes used to understand and solve problems. That alone, however, will not be sufficient for a successful transition to this model. Educational leaders must also identify, in advance, areas within their school system where the changes associated with the application of our framework will be a significant challenge. Following are some of the more common and problematic gaps between our framework and current practices, as well as strategies for addressing those discrepancies.

Where to Start—Introducing the Framework to Your School

During a recent consultation, a principal used a metaphor that was enlightening and shaped the way we now introduce our framework. He shared the following:

> I love mowing my lawn and am always looking on the internet to find new fertilizers and treatments to keep my grass green and thick. There's something gratifying

about eliminating the weeds, not having any brown spots in the yard, and mowing perfectly straight lines each week. The most important part, I have learned, is treating the soil so the grass can thrive but the weeds and crabgrass cannot. When I think about your framework, the Conditions for Change is like the soil, which needs to be in place before doing anything else.

Although our collective expertise does not extend to lawn care, the metaphor fits perfectly. As an educational leader, you need to actively cultivate the soil in your school environment to make sure the Conditions for Change are present and clearly visible to your teachers and staff. Before teachers can understand why it is so important to balance psychological safety and accountability, they need to know exactly what those terms mean and how you intend to prioritize them. This should include active discussions and modeling of desired actions and behaviors with explicit labeling. When a teacher introduces an innovative approach to foster social-emotional learning that fails to produce the expected results, it is critical to acknowledge that teacher's efforts and recognize that recycling mistakes and setbacks into learning is a critical component of psychological safety. The role of accountability looks different within our framework. Specifically, teachers must know that mistakes and failed lessons are acceptable, as long as they learn from them and adjust their approach to teaching accordingly. The lessons learned from mistakes and failures should also be shared with colleagues to promote successful practices throughout the system. Therefore, a punitive response or consequence for educators and staff members within our framework is reserved for those who fail to learn from their mistakes and continue to rely on ineffective practices.

Educational leaders must actively assess the sense of belonging and communication practices currently in place at their school, as discussed in Chapters 4 and 5, respectively. By listening for the quiet voice, providing teachers and staff multiple options for sharing feedback, and actively including all perspectives and, where possible, all voices in different initiatives, educational leaders can demonstrate the importance of be-longing and open, honest communication practices. It is equally important to identify when these conditions for change are lacking and investigate possible explanations for their absence. When staff meetings are met with overwhelming silence and lack of participation, educational leaders need to look at the data as an opportunity for growth and learning. Seek feedback from your teachers and staff to help identify and understand barriers to change. Most importantly, be sure to thank others for their willingness to communicate openly and honestly when they provide feedback. Do not disregard what they share—even when their perspective is inconsistent with your own.

Once Conditions for Change take root, you are ready to Apply the Framework referenced in Chapter 7. However, you must continue to monitor and treat the Conditions for Change to ensure educational practices have the soil in which to grow and thrive.

Here Comes the Pendulum—Fostering and Maintaining Engagement

Veteran educators grow weary and frustrated by new in-itiatives, questioning their longevity and the driving forces be-hind them. This is a common complaint from school-based teams and educational leaders with whom we have consulted over the years. Notable recurring themes include the introduc-tion of new curricula (i.e., both math and reading), social-emotional learning initiatives (i.e., how to fit them into the schedule and what to take out), response-to-intervention efforts (i.e., differentiating between regular and special education in-terventions), and district-wide initiatives to improve student learning (e.g., teams of administrators conducting instructional rounds). Given the fast-paced world of education, teachers and staff members have told us they often opt to wait-out the ex-citement behind new initiatives, assuming they will just fade away with time. This sense of apathy could be misinterpreted as a lack of commitment. But for many teachers and staff members who have worked in education for a long time, the Pendulum Effect (i.e., one waits out a new initiative anticipating something will replace it soon) is very real. It is critical that influential educational leaders avoid introducing the framework as a new initiative, or they run the risk of teachers and staff members becoming skeptical before it has a chance to be fully integrated.

Influential educational leaders should utilize the framework as a roadmap for creating an adaptive and nimble school culture that values multiple perspectives; recognizes the importance of surface-level, below-the-surface level, and systems-level contributions; and rests on the foundation of the conditions for change. Although we are not opposed to leaders sharing the roadmap with others, we believe walking-the-walk is more effective than talking-the-talk. Instead of sharing the framework with teachers and explaining that balancing psychological safety with accountability is one of the four conditions for change, educational leaders are encouraged to demonstrate how this idea comes alive in a real context. If a teacher acknowledges a lesson did not go well in a post-observation conference but is able to describe where learning was blocked and share ideas to work around those limitations, a supervisor should acknowledge this is the essence of how we learn and improve, thus applying the idea of psychological safety and accountability to the routine practice of supervision.

Passing Through the Portal—The Challenges of Open and Honest Communication

Engaging in open and honest communication is essential for positive change. Although universally accepted by educational leaders, it is a difficult paradigm shift for many school-based teams and school communities, especially when the small-diverse team (see Chapter 7) is convened to begin discussing the presenting problem facing the school.

When the team initially gathers, there often is skepticism about whether authentic honesty will be embraced. Often, it is not until "the anonymous survey" is conducted that someone shares something controversial or difficult to hear, such as a criticism of the principal or skepticism about the decision-making process. It is essential the group leader acknowledges the feelings and thoughts presented and gives everyone a chance to discuss their perspectives. The goal is to have all participants realize these meetings are places where they can openly and honestly discuss ideas. That doesn't mean all will agree. It is possible to acknowledge feelings on one hand but disagree with someone's perspective on the other. The goal is to establish a process where all ideas can be discussed openly; not to determine if the criticism is valid.

Avoiding normative social influence (Chapter 4) is essential to maintain open and honest communication. When discussing parent perceptions about the safety of children returning to school in the fall of 2020 due to COVID-19, for example, if the first parent response indicates significant concerns and a strong preference for remote learning, normative social influence suggests additional responses are more likely to be in agreement to avoid confrontation or conflict. Therefore, it is important to validate the initial position or sentiment expressed but also to invite dissenting opinions, acknowledging there are likely opposing viewpoints to be considered prior to making any final decision. A consistent lack of disagreement likely indicates the goal of open and honest communication has not been met for the group.

When Perspectives Collide—The Blame Game

Most educators are extremely dedicated individuals who invest incredible amounts of time and energy to their work. When they experience blame or criticism for that work, they can become defensive, which is understandable. Defensiveness limits the group's willingness to provide constructive feedback and the ability to improve as the result of lessons learned from mistakes and difficult conversations following disagreements. It is appropriate for targets of criticism to describe their feelings. It is also vital they realize having the criticism out in the open allows for the sharing of different perspectives. That is impossible when criticism stays underground. A program director for students with emotional and behavioral challenges shared the following after receiving constructive feedback about the struggling program:

> It is hard for me to hear these criticisms because I have worked so hard to develop this program, and these students and their families have been so challenging to work with over the last couple of years. I have tried so many different approaches and feel like I have gone way above and beyond to increase family involvement, including visiting students' homes and communicating with families on weekends and during school vacations. A lot of my students live in group homes or foster homes, and there are so many collateral providers that sometimes it's hard to keep everything straight. So, I guess because I know how hard I'm working, it's hard to have someone tell me that parts of the program are not working or could be working better, even though I know it's true. I appreciate your willingness to share this perspective with me, however, because it allows me to reflect on it and share where I agree and where I might have a different perspective.

This kind of reaction can propel groups forward. Educators are more likely to respond this way when the goal of difficult conversations is clearly linked to improvement rather than blame. Educational leaders can tell teachers and staff the "blame game" no longer has a place at their schools. But it will take multiple experiences and time for that to become a reality.

Taking Selfies, and Responsibility

The most critical point for small and diverse groups comes when honesty starts to be embraced and the pain and challenges of the "blame game" begin to fade. Groups can easily get stuck there. The results will be reasonably good, but not necessarily great. To push through and achieve authentic insight into the strategies necessary for potent and durable solutions, groups need to examine how they, as representatives of the larger faculty, might also be contributing to the problem. This separates mediocrity from greatness. Achieving this requires that individuals be vulnerable and share ways their own beliefs and/or fears might limit embracing alternative pathways. Simply put, group members must answer the question, "In what way am I contributing to the problem?"

For some, it might be admitting their perception that attending their school's child study team is a waste of time. For others, it might be sharing their worry that disagreeing with a colleague's approach at a meeting will hurt that person's feelings. Regardless of one's contribution, including a step in the framework requiring self-reflection is extremely important. Explaining to all group members that each of them contributes to the problem in some way removes the option to opt out of this part of the conversation.

Usually there is someone in a diverse team willing to share something that kicks off this phase of the discussion. Once that person shares their contribution to the problem, the leader should acknowledge the courage it took to share insights and the help it provides. If there are no volunteers willing to share their contribution to the problem, leaders have three options. First, they can model what this sounds like by sharing their perceptions of how they contribute to the problem. Knowing this is possible and even likely when the framework is first implemented, leaders have the advantage of preparing in advance. Secondly, group leaders can stress the importance of identifying and sharing how group members contribute to the problem and end discussions temporarily to give members time to prepare their responses or to respond anonymously after the meeting. Finally, knowing this is a challenging but important step in the framework, group leaders could ask members to discuss why this is such a challenging question to talk about with each other. While not directly responding to the contribution question, this discussion could uncover important factors blocking dialogue.

Really Dealing with Emotions and Feelings

Chapter 2 covers how unexpressed feelings often leak out into behaviors. This is why the Below-the-Surface dimension (e.g., emotions and feelings) is so important and why educational leaders must look beyond the actions and behaviors of teachers and staff members and, as written by Brackett (2019), give them "Permission to Feel." Bracket shared when he asks attendees at his seminars what would be different in a world where everyone was taught emotion skills and trained to value emotional intelligence, numerous responses were shared. The following eight responses are relevant to schools and our framework for influential educational leaders (pp. 239–240):

1. Everyone would listen more and judge less.
2. Feelings would be seen as strengths, not weaknesses.
3. More people would be their authentic, best selves.
4. Emotional intelligence would be as important to education as math, literacy, and science.
5. Schools would be places where students spend time reflecting on their purpose and passion and developing the skills they need to make their dreams come true.
6. People would leave their workplace thinking, I can't wait to return tomorrow.
7. There would be less bullying, a greater sense of belonging, and more harmonious relationships.
8. Families and schools would work together to support kids' healthy development.

Given the potential benefits of actively and intentionally including emotions and feelings in our framework, educational leaders must be prepared to respond to and manage the emotions of others and the group as a whole during discussions and meetings. To be clear, the goal is not to suppress emotions, as that would be counterproductive. Instead, the goal of group leaders should be to help others identify and express their emotions and feelings in a way that helps groups develop a better understanding of the problems or challenges they are facing. When emotions and feelings become personal or damaging to the group process, the role of group leaders should be to validate those feelings but also redirect conversations to the emotions related to the problem under discussion.

Since many school cultures do not promote talking about emotions and feelings, Brackett (2019) suggests leaders should model discussing their emotions and feelings with others to make it clear their school is a safe place for those conversations. A colleague worked as a school psychologist for years and never felt valued because his office was next to the gym, resulting in constant noise and disruptions during testing and counseling sessions. Since he did not feel comfortable sharing his feelings and emotions, the lack of value he experienced leaked out into his behaviors. He stopped volunteering for extra committees, rarely attended after-school and evening events, and ultimately left the district. Had talking about emotions and feelings been a regular practice actively encouraged by leaders at his school, perhaps he would have felt more comfortable talking about his feelings of not being valued, which might have resulted in a new office and a longer tenure for him there. Since the structure and routines were not in place to discuss his emotions and feelings, the problem remained unidentified and, therefore, unaddressed. The psychologist's lack of connection to the school and sense of belonging ultimately resulted in him leaving.

Surviving Setbacks/Failures, and Thriving Because of Them

When schools moved to online instruction in March 2020, teachers, principals, and central office administrators developed plans and strategies to support this transition. Teachers, who for the most part had never done this before, had to execute plans, conforming their own styles and interests to the expectations of their leaders. How well did these approaches work? Do we know? Did we collect any data from our teachers, students, or parents? Variability is a significant part of any initiative. Failure to focus on variability leaves us unable to determine which approaches worked well, which were satisfactory, and which ones failed. There are many reasons we rarely collect such data. Sometimes it simply is because we fail to recognize its importance. Other times, we are reluctant to collect data because it might not be positive (i.e., it might suggest our hard work was not effective). And still other times, we are not sure what data to collect. The application of our framework can falter if the teams do not spend time soliciting data from key constituencies about the impact of strategies or approaches utilized.

This may not necessitate a rigorous quantitative analysis. It may be as simple as asking students, teachers, or parents for their observations and impressions. In every school district, there were teachers with approaches to remote student learning that worked well and showed promising results. Do we know who these teachers were? Do we know what they did to personalize their approach? Without such information, we are approaching our next iteration of online teaching without insight. While there are a number of ways to collect data, we have found the diverse team assembled to study the problem and develop a set of approaches to solve it is often an effective group to collect information about how the recommended approaches are working.

Racing the Clock—If We Only Had More Time

The final challenge to applying the framework to an actual school environment is far too common and very real. The pace at which schools and educators function is often somewhere between frantic and hyper-speed. Given all of the moving parts at each level of education, introducing new initiatives or frameworks certainly can feel overwhelming. At the elementary level, teachers manage classrooms of 20 to 30 students, differentiating instruction throughout the curriculum, keeping track of all support staff coming in and out of the classroom, and creating a classroom climate that is both challenging and emotionally attuned and supportive. Secondary teachers often teach well over 150 students per day, in various subjects and differing levels of complexity. They often have additional responsibilities within their departments, are involved with extracurricular activities for students, or have coaching commitments at their schools. Asking educators to work more, attend more meetings, and help solve systemic problems is not often feasible.

The goal of the framework, however, is not to add work or responsibilities to the overflowing plates of educators. Instead, the framework ultimately changes the culture of the school community so problems can be solved and challenges met more consistently and efficiently. Although executing the steps as delineated in Chapter 7, A Leadership Guide—Moving from Theory to Practice, does require time and effort, this comprehensive approach is not necessary, or even recommended, for a majority of the daily obstacles for learning encountered by educational leaders. Pulling together a diverse team of stakeholders is unnecessary for a building principal trying to decide on a presenter for the upcoming professional development day, the lunch schedule for elementary students, or selecting the best platform for remote learning in the fall. The framework and action steps work best at solving significant problems at the school or district level: What should the professional development goals be for the school community over the next few years? Should school nutrition be a target for change in the district? What should the school reopening plan be in the fall? In this broader realm, the framework and action steps are critical.

Following are two case studies that illustrate the impact of the framework and the sequence of the recommended steps in action. By providing examples at both the elementary and secondary levels, we hope the application will resonate with readers from all levels of education.

Reference

Brackett, M. (2019). *Permission to feel: Unlocking the power of emotions to help our kids, ourselves, and our society thrive.* Celadon Books.

9

Case Study 1: Student Placement

Introduction

This first vignette focuses on the student placement process—a common problem for elementary school leaders. Every year in late spring, elementary educators discuss what their classrooms should look like the following year. Although the process varies from one school to the next, the problem facing many teachers and principals is the same. Many teachers have long-standing reputations for being very strong or very weak with specific student populations. These reputations often influence the student placement process, as teams are reluctant to place students with challenging behaviors with teachers who struggle to connect with and/or support "that kind of student." As a result, "stronger" teachers often end up with more challenging classrooms, while "weaker" teachers end up with fewer challenging students. The cycle continues year after year. This was the case when Ms. McGowan, an elementary school principal in a large suburban school district, asked us to consult with her school to revise the student placement process to make it more equitable.

Meeting 1: Identifying the Problem

The goal of our first meeting with Principal McGowan was simply to better understand the problem to determine how our framework could improve the student placement process at her school. We asked her to explain the current process, how it developed, and the rationale behind it from her perspective. Her response was a common one for many school leaders. Ms. McGowan was in her fourth year as principal after being a teacher in the district for eight years. The current student placement process had been in place for as long as she could remember, and the familiarity and comfort of the routine had not changed much over the years. Although minor changes had been introduced, such as using colored sticky notes for each student or separating students into three tiers of ability to balance classrooms, no major changes had been discussed or implemented. She added, "It has always been on my list of things to change at the school, but when May rolls around, things are just too busy. It's just easier to keep the process the same. It's one of the initiatives that keeps waiting until next year." We talked briefly about distribution of effort to help Principal McGowan recognize why changing the system can be challenging. The idea of spending so much time on maintenance and putting out fires clearly resonated with her, but she reiterated her commitment to revising the student placement process because she felt problems were growing and taking a toll on her "stronger" teachers.

Principal McGowan explained that she usually has three classrooms at each grade level, kindergarten through fifth grade. There has not been a great deal of teacher movement over the years, but the school usually adds one or two teachers to staff each year. Some grade-level teams are stronger than others; two in particular have been in place for over ten years. Most of the teachers are very familiar with the placement process, and it mostly runs on autopilot each May. Equally predictable are teacher complaints about specific teachers avoiding students with challenging behaviors, families who are hard to work with, students with comprehensive IEPs because their schedules are too disruptive, or students who are lower functioning because "they often struggle in my classroom." The complaints are the same each year but are only expressed in whispers or during infamous parking lot conversations.

Principal McGowan felt the resentment had been building for too long, and a new recommendation from one of her veteran teachers made it clear it was time for a major change. The recommendation was a simple one: Build all classroom lists for the following year and make them as balanced as possible—then randomly assign teachers to the lists. This was the student placement version of "You get what you get, and you don't get upset." Although she knew the shift would not be that easy, Principal McGowan was committed to improving the process for all teachers and families. She wanted to change the system and asked for our help to do so.

Meeting 2: Anticipating the Four Perspectives

We started the second meeting by asking Principal McGowan how the different groups of stakeholders from the school community would react to changing the student placement process. We shared the Four Perspectives from our framework and asked her to think about responses from the district administrative team, her teachers, and students and families. We also explained a critical step in our framework included speaking to representatives from each stakeholder group directly to ensure their perspective was expressed and considered when it came time to brainstorm and implement changes.

The Superintendent Perspective

Principal McGowan started with the superintendent, sharing that he has only been involved in these kinds of discussions when there have been problems. In those rare situations, parents typically schedule an appointment with the superintendent and demand their child be moved out of their current classroom because (a) they didn't get the teacher they wanted, (b) the student does not have any friends in the classroom, (c) the teacher is not meeting the parent's expectations in some way, or (d) the student is having problems with other kids in the classroom. The superintendent typically hears the parent out and promises to follow-up with Principal McGowan to get more information.

When they eventually meet to discuss the situation, the super-intendent's preference is to move the student right away—thus eliminating the problem, keeping it small, and hoping to foster parent support in the community. Although he is open other solutions, his preference is clear, and moving students is common. Principal McGowan explained the superintendent told her over the years, "Sometimes we need to use geography to solve the problem."

The Principal Perspective

We then explained to Principal McGowan how important her perspective, as the leader of the school, would be in changing the way the system manages the student placement process. We asked her to articulate her vision for the new process and identify her priorities. We explained how important it will be moving forward for her to share her vision and priorities with the other stakeholder groups. She shared the following:

> My vision is to establish a new process for student placement at our school that is completely transparent, places our students in classrooms so they can thrive, and challenges our teachers to continue growing as profes-sionals so they are able to provide an excellent educa-tional environment to all students. I also want to make sure our teachers, students, and families know support is available to all of them when problems arise. We know problems will arise when we introduce this new approach to student placement.

The Teacher Perspective

Ms. McGowan shared with us that her biggest concern was how teachers would respond. She knew there would be two strong opposing viewpoints on changing the process for student pla-cement. First, the majority of teachers would support the change because they felt the current system was broken, and some teachers often had easier classrooms because they struggled with specific kinds of students. A smaller group of teachers would be opposed to change, feeling it would be a set-up for them to get students and families who were already "out to get them." As the conversation continued, Principal McGowan started to question how many of her teachers would respond to the new process. Fortunately, we told her our next step in the framework would help us figure that out.

The Family Perspective

Principal McGowan was surprised to hear us ask about the student and family perspective, as she felt the decision should be made at the school level. She was reluctant to involve parents and families in discussions about student placement. We explained we were not asking students and families to make decisions; rather we were asking what she thought their perspective would be should they join the conversation at some point. Principal McGowan felt parents would want more influence in choosing teachers and/or classrooms, especially when it came to making sure their children had friends in their classrooms. She also felt fortunate to have so many strong grade-level teams, meaning a majority of her families rarely complained about placement. Finally, she acknowledged she was unsure what many of her parents would say about changing the classroom placement process, as many of them were not aware of how the current process worked in the first place.

Creating a Small and Diverse Committee

Following our discussion with Principal McGowan about the four perspectives, we talked with her about the importance of developing a small (8–12 people), diverse committee of stakeholders that would work collaboratively to help change the student placement process at her school. We suggested the following composition:

◆ Ms. McGowan, Principal
◆ Three classroom teachers from different grade-levels with different views on student placement
◆ Two specialist teachers (e.g., physical education, art, music)

- ◆ Two members of the special education team
- ◆ Two parents

We reminded her to consider issues related to gender, race, and socio-economic status (SES) to ensure her committee would be diverse in backgrounds, as well as perspectives.

Meeting 3: Meeting with the Committee

The third meeting included the committee that Principal McGowan constructed to help the school change the student placement process. The target number of 10 grew to 12 when a third member of the special education team asked to join and a third parent volunteered for the committee. We asked Principal McGowan to provide an overview of the current system, as well as her concerns about it to the group. We then asked her to share her priorities for the new process but requested she not propose any solutions at this time. We challenged the group to share their perspectives in an open and honest way and to really listen to one another without judgment. We shared the following guidelines with the group and invited questions from the participants to ensure they understood the process:

1. **Be Present:** This means more than just be in attendance. It means you are an important part of the group, your perspective matters and needs to be shared with others, and you will share your perspective in a respectful, nonjudgmental manner.
2. **Be Accurate and Truthful:** Others in the group are depending on you to understand your part in the system. Share your concerns, stressors, feelings, and experiences. Share your voice and your voice alone. Do not speak for others.
3. **Be a Good Listener:** Be open to the experiences of others and know they are likely different from your own. Understand others may not agree with you but still

have pure motives. Remember the goal of the initial conversation is to clearly define the problem—not solve it.

4. **Be Reflective:** Actively ask yourself before, during, and after the group conversation how you might be contributing to the problem. There is a major difference between contributing to the problem and causing the problem.

Committee members then ask a few questions. One of the parents from the group asks about confidentiality, wanting to ensure concerns expressed during conversations will not be shared outside the group. All agree it will be extremely important to maintain confidentiality. A teacher then shares her concern about the discussion becoming too personal, noting she feels uncomfortable listening to others criticize her colleagues. Group members agrees to share concerns in general terms, not questioning or criticizing specific parents, teachers, children, or administrators. Finally, a teacher from the special education team requests the conversation also consider the impact of classroom placement on specialists throughout the building. All members agree specialist schedules are an important part of the conversation. When reflecting on the experience later, this specialist felt this moment was the most powerful, validating part of the entire process for her. Once the group was comfortable with the guidelines, they began to share their perspectives about the classroom placement process at the school.

As facilitators of the discussion, we took notes at the meeting and invited comments from different perspectives less represented in the flow of conversation. We reminded committee members of the guidelines on several occasions and let them know mistakes are common when new to the framework. The most common mistakes are rushing to problem-solving (i.e., *solutionitis* from Bryk, Gomez, Grunow, & LeMahieu, 2015) and questioning and/or disagreeing with experiences of others. Following a few reminders, which were often followed by laughter by the group, these missteps were eliminated. The conversation lasted approximately one hour, and the primary contributions from each stakeholder group included the following.

The school administrator perspective presented by Principal McGowan focused on making sure teachers and families were both happy with student placements and students were placed in classrooms in which they could thrive. She also shared she was confident in a majority of the placement decisions made each year, but could easily predict within minutes of reviewing the proposed lists which placements were going to be problematic and which teachers and families were most likely to express concerns. She acknowledged occasionally moving students to avoid the challenging conversations and meetings with parents and teachers that would likely follow, saying she does not feel good about it because it only promotes discontent throughout the school community. Finally, she shared that once problems escalate to the superintendent, students almost always end up getting moved.

The teacher perspective was well represented on the committee with three classroom teachers, two specialist teachers, and three members of the special education team. The prevailing sentiment expressed by the teachers was that the placement process had been broken for a long time, and they were excited to be part of the change. Their concerns included some teachers being "protected" from taking challenging students and/or families, while others were consistently asked to take on a disproportionate number of challenging students and/or families because they are "good with those kinds of kids and families." Finally, one brave teacher shared she would be more comfortable having a challenging student and/or family on her list if she genuinely believed she would be supported when vulnerable. Someone asked what she meant by "vulnerable." She responded by saying:

> In general, I have a hard time with aggressive students and families. I'm not always comfortable with conflict, and defiant behavior has always been hard for me to manage. I tend to put on my authoritarian hat too quickly, and often rely on the principal or vice principal to fix the problem for me. One of my third grade colleagues is great with those kinds of kids, and their

families always love her, so I have a feeling a lot of those students end up in her room for a reason. If we are going to change the placement process, and if I am going to have more challenging students in my classroom, it will be extremely important to me that I have support and people understand I am likely to make mistakes.

Finally, the parent perspective was well-represented by three parents with children in various grades at the school. One quickly shared, "It seems like all of the room parents get to choose their teachers, and their kids always have tons of friends in their classes every year. For those of us not able to be room parents because we work or simply don't feel comfortable in that role, it feels really unfair." Although it was hard for teachers and Principal McGowan to not disagree or explain-away the "misperception" of the parent who shared, we reminded them of the guidelines, and the conversation continued. The parent comments reflected parents mostly were satisfied with the teacher placement process and had no idea how much time and energy went into making the lists each year. One final parent comment resonated with Principal McGowan and teachers when the parent asked, "What happened to Step-Up Day? The kids used to get so excited to meet their new teachers and see which kids were going to be in their classroom. It always felt like a really fun way to end the school year. Then it ended, and no one really knew why that tradition did not continue."

The meeting ended after the group was reminded about the time and date of the next meeting. Each participant was asked to complete a short survey about the meeting that would ask for honest assessment about the effectiveness of the meeting and the degree to which the team was acting on the assumptions with fidelity, as well as provide each person an opportunity to share something they did not say at the meeting but wanted to share with the group. Principal McGowan said that while the survey was anonymous, she would share the results with the whole team at the beginning of the next meeting so everyone could discuss the "data" from the survey.

Meeting 4: Verify the Problem Statement

Principal McGowan began by summarizing the anonymous feedback from the previous meeting. It was limited—mostly positive comments about feeling valued and appreciating the opportunity to participate in the group. Two responses stood out and were read aloud. The first was: "If we are being honest, there is some truth to the concern some parents get the teachers they want because teachers talk. It's nice to have families in your classroom you know will support you and be positive. I'm not sure if this is a good thing or not, but if our goal is to be transparent, I thought this should be part of the conversation." Principal McGowan asked the group to reflect prior to responding and proceeded to read the second note saying, "Parents talk to each other and to the teachers, and some parents do everything they can to get the teacher they want for the next year. To be honest, I've done it too. It's just so important for kids to have positive school experiences in elementary school." As the group considered the feedback, Principal McGowan shared a draft of the problem statement she wrote based on the group's discussion from the previous meeting.

> The current process for creating classroom rosters at our school needs updating and revising. The new process should still seek to create balanced classrooms, but the role of parent and teacher preferences should be significantly reduced. Instead of assigning students with certain profiles to the same teachers repeatedly because they are "good with those kinds of kids," all teachers should be expected to work well with all types of students. For this to work, we need to actively support our teachers who are being asked to work with an increasingly-diverse population of students and families. By creating a more transparent process, we also need a commitment from our families to be supportive partners with teachers and the school and understanding when challenges arise.

With a few minor changes, the group endorsed the problem statement, which was then shared with the entire faculty via email. Teachers and staff members were asked to provide feedback to the committee, and the statement was revised accordingly. The final draft looked very similar to the initial one written by Principal McGowan.

Meeting 5: Mapping the Contribution System

Problem statement in hand, the group reconvened to discuss factors that contributed to the difficulties associated with student placement. Energized by the previous meetings, the group had found a good rhythm. Their ensuing conversation identified the following contributions.

First, the superintendent's direct role in student placement had been minimal. When he does get involved, students typically get moved. Therefore, the group agreed the superintendent is indirectly contributing to the problem by reinforcing parent behaviors and establishing a precedent that when parents request a meeting with him, their child will get moved. Therefore, the group decided inviting the superintendent to join one of their meetings would be an important next step. His perspective would be important to include, and his support of the new process would be critical in determining its success. Although the superintendent declined to join the meeting, he did agree to meet with Principal McGowan to hear about the new process once it was finalized.

Second, the principal's role in student placement was critical. The process had not changed since Principal McGowan took over, and many teachers were looking for her to get more involved. Principal McGowan suggested one way she was contributing to the problem was by not prioritizing the need for change. After further discussion, one of the specialists suggested holding teachers accountable for adjusting their style to meet the needs of the kids would be important if the new process was implemented. A difficult conversation ensued, but all parties eventually agreed accountability was sometimes lacking for teachers, a valuable lesson for Principal McGowan that she later acknowledged was an opportunity for improvement.

Third, the teacher role was critical for several reasons. The most important being all teachers were well aware of the flawed student placement process but had not made any authentic efforts to change it. There were a lot of "parking lot" conversations that included complaining about colleagues who never seemed to have "hard kids" in their rooms, but that data was never used to influence change. In fact, those conversations passively reinforced the problems, as they created divisions between teachers, sometimes within grade-level teams. Instead of supporting one another in the interest of improvement and building capacity, the isolated complaining continuously reinforced the perceptions some teachers could not successfully teach students with certain profiles.

At this point in the conversation we, as consultants, reminded the group about the importance of open and honest communication and its connection to psychological safety. With our ability to view the system as outsiders, we suggested open and honest communication was inconsistently present within the school and often disappeared when challenging conversations and uncomfortable moments presented themselves. We suggested the balance between psychological safety and accountability may be a little off, resulting in the school falling into the "Comfort Zone" at times (Edmondson, 2019). Finally, we shared that these two challenges are extremely common in schools and for principals early on in their careers.

Parent representatives were eager to share their contributions. (Note: We often find the group sharing last is the most prepared and comfortable responding. The final group benefits from observing self-reflection from the other groups, which helps foster a sense of belonging and openness cultivating rich discussions). The parent contributions, which they had written down for the group, included (a) attempting to indirectly influence the student placement process and (b) not having an open mind when their children were not placed with the teacher they hoped.

Meeting 6: Creating a Plan for Action and Evaluation

The group reconvened for a final meeting to discuss a new student placement plan. Principal McGowan started by reviewing some of the main points from the previous meetings and shared the final version of the problem statement. She then invited members to share their ideas for improving the process, which she wrote on a whiteboard. The group ultimately agreed to the following new plan for student placement:

1. Balanced classroom rosters would be created by current teachers for the following year without assigning teachers.
2. The following variables would be balanced as much possible across each grade: Gender, students on IEPs, three broad categories of academic achievement (high, medium, and low), and behavior problems. Ethnicity was also discussed, but the lack of diversity at the school made this a difficult variable to balance without leaving children of color feeling culturally isolated. Ultimately, Principal McGowan said she would talk to the district's Director of Diversity and Inclusion and solicit feedback on this issue.
3. Student rosters would be shared with Principal McGowan, who would then meet with classroom teachers for the following year to review the lists. Teachers were encouraged to collaborate to determine who would take each class, and the principal would remain a passive participant in the conversation, intervening only when needed.
4. Once the teachers were assigned to classroom rosters, each teacher was given one week to review their list and prepare for an individual meeting with Principal McGowan, who would ask each teacher the same question: What can I do to support you in preparation for next year?
5. Principal McGowan agreed to have an active presence in classrooms to start the school year and to schedule

meetings with each teacher after the first month of school to offer support or resources, as needed.

6. The plan would be announced to the entire school community so families would understand the process. In addition, parent representatives from the committee would share their experiences with the PTO and strongly recommend parents not attempt to influence placement decisions.

7. Finally, the superintendent agreed to support the new process for the upcoming school year and decided he would invite Principal McGowan to join any meetings with parents from her school when discussions involved student placement. They both agreed to revisit the plan at the end of the school year to determine if it was effective, and, if so, if it should be replicated at other schools in the district.

Although a written summary rarely captures every detail, emotion, or conflict occurring in real life, we hope this step-by-step vignette is helpful for understanding our proposed framework for educational leaders. As in the student placement vignette, we consistently find Conditions for Change play a critical role when teams come together to solve problems within the school system. Fortunately, this also means improving Conditions for Change will address other problems within the system that have not yet been identified. In this case, Principal McGowan's realization that her school was operating in the "Comfort Zone" led her to revisit her process for conducting teacher evaluations.

Ultimately, this is the goal of the framework and the reason we are sharing it with educational leaders. The Conditions for Change are at the center of our framework and serve as the foundation for learning in school environments. Learning should never be limited to the students, as each group of stakeholders, represented by the four perspectives, must keep working to improve and evolve as the demands and challenges for schools continue to change. Finally, our framework requires school leaders to recognize and pay attention to the actions and behaviors of others, but to always remember they represent emotions and feelings and are directly influenced by invisible forces within the system. When educational leaders truly understand how the framework works and can be applied to their schools, they will be in position to maximize their influence to create a school community that is constantly adapting, learning, and improving so students can thrive.

References

Bryk, A. S., Gomez, L. M., Grunow, A., & LeMahieu, P. G. (2015). *Learning to improve: How America's schools can get better and getting better.* Harvard Education Press.

Edmondson, A. C. (2019). *The fearless organization: Creating psychological safety in the workplace for learning, innovation, and growth.* Wiley and Sons.

10

Case Study 2: COVID-19, Returning to School

Introduction

Principal Rodney Jones of Westminster High School wanted to assemble a team to help him prepare for school reopening in fall 2020. He assembled a diverse team of stakeholders including a member from each academic department, two parents from the school council, the president of the senior class, the union president, one of two assistant principals, and a member of the student services department. Counting himself, the team had 14 members. Principal Jones explained to the team that he wanted them to dive deeply into uncovering the challenges they would have to meet and overcome once school reopens. He went on to say he wanted to separate technical challenges related to safety protocols from instructional and social/emotional factors that a return to school requires. The team, he said, would focus solely on instructional and social/emotional factors. He did not want the team to start brainstorming ways to meet reopening challenges without first anticipating what they would likely be. He hoped the team would fully "diagnose" the problem (i.e., obstacles and barriers limiting a smooth and effective reopening) first.

Principal Jones knew this would not be easy. Team members held a variety of different perspectives which influenced their recommendations for the school's reopening plan. Some wanted school to return to regular routines and practices as quickly as possible; others felt the pandemic offered an opportunity to re-structure and rethink how we "do school." Still others worried unequal student experiences under quarantine would significantly impact their social and emotional development, as well as widen the academic gap that existed prior to the pandemic.

Meeting 1: Sharing Assumptions and Identifying the Problem

Principal Jones thanked group members for their willingness to participate in this important work. He explained the work would be divided into two phases. Phase I would focus on understanding the problem or the challenges they would en-counter. Phase II would consist of brainstorming strategies to counteract or resolve the anticipated problems. During each phase, Principal Jones explained that the group would share its work with the full faculty and PTO and ask for feedback about possible factors they might have missed or left out. He then distributed the assumptions recommended by Schwarz (2016) that he wanted to guide their work. They include:

- ◆ I have information; so do other people.
- ◆ Each of us sees things others don't.
- ◆ People may disagree with me and still have pure motives.
- ◆ Differences are opportunities for learning.
- ◆ How might I be contributing to the problem?

After giving the group time to read through the assumptions, he assigned pairs to share their thoughts. Finally, he brought group members back together and asked if anything about the assumptions was unclear. Someone asked how to define "pure motives." Principal Jones explained that sometimes when people share perspectives that are different, people do not just assess their ideas but sometimes question their motivation.

He said that he wanted the group to accept the assumption that the content of an idea was what needed to be discussed without fear of being judged for having nefarious motives. Someone else asked for clarification on the meaning of "contributing to the problem." Principal Jones shared that organizations where people were willing to examine how they themselves might be contributing to an issue or problem had a better chance of achieving significant improvements. He went on to explain that sometimes our own fears or worries about succeeding lead us to reject strategies that might be more effective in the long run. His explanations allowed for sufficient understanding and enabled the group to move forward.

Principal Jones asked group members if they would be willing to adhere to the assumptions. All agreed. He went on to say he would send out an anonymous survey at the end of each meeting asking for an honest assessment about the effectiveness of the meeting, the degree to which the team was acting on the assumptions with fidelity, and providing an opportunity for each person to share something they did not voice at the meeting but wanted to share with the group. He said he would share the results of the anonymous survey with the whole team at the beginning of the next meeting so everyone could discuss the "data" collected.

For the next 15 minutes, the group explored important issues that present barriers to a smooth reopening. Some ideas generated were:

- ◆ Reconnecting with the students and finding out what the quarantine experience was like for them.
- ◆ Assessing for and responding to any trauma students and families might have experienced (e.g., food scarcity, loss of jobs, loss of loved ones).
- ◆ Assessing learning gaps and the potential "COVID slump."
- ◆ Acknowledging and discussing the inequities COVID highlighted.
- ◆ Morale of teachers; reconnecting with staff; what the experience was like for them.

◆ What, if anything, do we want to retain from distant learning strategies used during spring and summer 2020?

◆ Teachers' fears about returning to school—capture their emotions.

◆ Reconnecting with parents; understanding their experiences; soliciting their feedback for future reference.

The meeting ended with a statement about the time and date of the next meeting and a reminder to fill out the survey.

Meeting 2: Defining the Problem, Welcoming Emotions

Data collected from the first survey indicated the participants felt the initial meeting was well run and members acted in accordance with the assumptions. One person wrote he/she was unsure the principal and other team members would accept complete honesty in the group. This gave Principal Jones a chance to reiterate he would be open to all thoughts and observations. He emphasized the problem they sought to address did not have any blueprint to follow and that most schools really were struggling to create a reopening plan. Getting as many ideas on the table as possible for the team to consider would be critical.

Further discussion ensued about obstacles about which people worried. One person asked about expectations for work: Should our expectations be the same? Whether homework, projects, or the number of concepts covered in class, should we proceed at the same pacing we once had? Members responded quickly to those questions. The principal interjected, thanking members for their energy and reminding them to stick with the diagnosing the problem first. He noted that "pacing" was one issue needing to be addressed.

Someone else shared that another challenge would be doing more with less due to state funding shortfalls. They anticipated cuts and reductions in staffing and supplies would be likely, given the massive negative impact of COVID-19 on our economy. They continued pointing out that hundreds of teachers across the state were laid off in spring 2020 and were still waiting to find out if they would be rehired. This made planning for the reopening even more challenging.

A parent spoke at this point saying she hoped all students would receive specific and detailed feedback about their learning progress when school reopened. She further explained how disappointed she was with the quality of feedback many students received (having spoken to a number of parents), saying feedback was often general and vague. At this point, the president of the union spoke about how upset many teachers were about the many criticisms they received during the quarantine, despite what he described were heroic efforts to convert teaching to distant learning with little or no warning and limited professional development. Principal Jones interjected, acknowledging he appreciated the strong feelings and perspectives shared and noting he did not want anyone to feel somebody is right and somebody is wrong. He continued saying there were strong feelings on both sides. Parents desired more feedback, and teachers wanted more understanding and appreciation for the significant challenges they faced transitioning to distant learning. He wondered aloud, "What can we learn from this exchange that could inform our re-entry plan?"

Someone mentioned that perhaps they needed to figure out a way of sharing feelings but also asking for understanding and acknowledgment, rather than judgment. Someone else asked, "How should we capture that so it can be added to the list of items we need to think about?" After a period of silence, someone said perhaps they could create a placeholder and, for now, call it "Acknowledgment and Healing Sessions." The principal ended the meeting thanking members for their participation and acknowledging that feelings ran high towards the end of the meeting. He shared his deep appreciation that members were willing to share their worries and concern, noting it was a little uncomfortable, but better than keeping those feelings to themselves.

Meeting 3: Self-Reflection, Leading by Example

The survey from the previous meeting indicated group members again thought that the meeting was worthwhile and that people were following the assumptions. One person noted that he thought the principal had cut off the exchange between the parent and union president too quickly. Another person wrote he thought others should have been invited to speak on the topic raised by the parent. Both items were discussed briefly, and Principal Jones acknowledged both suggestions were worthy and that he, too, wondered whether he should have facilitated differently. One person spoke up and said she appreciated his openness to feedback and was not sure continuing that conversation would have been beneficial, saying she thought he had kept the group focused on the task at hand. The group moved on to review their list of factors and start preparing for a brief faculty meeting to update staff about their work and request input.

With 15 minutes left, the principal asked how well they were addressing the assumption, "How might I be contributing to the problem?" He asked members to think about ways their own actions might contribute to the challenges of a smooth reopening. Most looked puzzled. Someone asked if Principal Jones was asking about ways teachers might impede a smooth reopening? Tensions rose in the group. Principal Jones responded saying they all might be contributing in ways they might not be consciously aware. He shared that he knew he had not done enough to appreciate the pressures teachers were under in taking care of their own families while trying to create a distant learning program. He went on to say he thought his lack of acknowledgment might have left some feeling angry or hurt. This statement lessened the tension in the room and cleared the air. Bringing up the topic, especially around what many consider a taboo subject (i.e., staff concerns about his leadership during the quarantine period), felt like a fresh breeze.

One teacher spoke up and thanked him. Another suggested he should share that reflection at the upcoming staff meeting.

Before the meeting ended, Principal Jones shared that the next agenda would be to finalize the list of issues to be tackled in Phase II and to incorporate any feedback received at the faculty meeting.

Meeting 4: Belonging and Communication

The survey from the third meeting did not indicate any significant criticisms. Quite a few acknowledged the power of hearing the principal's nondefensive self-examination. Two participants shared how they might be contributing to the problem. One wrote that her anxiety about mastering technology prevented her from using tools that could benefit her students upon their return, as well as a possible return to quarantine. The person wrote, "I am a confident, experienced teacher, but during quarantine, I felt like a novice again. I was embarrassed about how little knowledge I had about Zoom or other tools, and, worse yet, I didn't think I could learn these tools effectively and quickly. I guess I realized that I saw myself as an old dog who couldn't learn new tricks." Another member mentioned that she found herself feeling she did not know how to keep students focused and engaged in an online environment. She acknowledged her one-on-one conferences with students went well, as did her small group engagements. But her whole class engagements felt boring and uninspiring. She mused that she is now wondering if Zoom revealed more clearly how her face-to-face classes were going all the while and that, perhaps, she needs to think about how to shift her regular instruction into a more personalized, small group format—a thought which terrified her.

Principal Jones thanked the group for completing the survey and said that while he did not know who wrote those statements, he was both appreciative of their honesty and guessed they might not be the only ones feeling that way. One of the parents spoke next and said that she had two children at home—one in 5th and one in 7th grade. She said that her 5th grader was self-directed in his learning in ways that surprised and pleased her, but her older child needed to be prodded, reminded, and at times yelled at in order to get him engaged. She worried she had directed his activities and choices more than her younger child, leaving him few choices. She worried this kind of directedness and control left him not knowing how to learn when no one was telling him what to do. She hoped educators could help him develop more energy and motivation to pursue learning, not just out of compliance, but out of desire. She thought it would better prepare him, not only for a possible return to quarantine, but also for life.

Principal Jones sensed something had shifted within the group at this point and shared his gut feeling. One person named it saying that she deeply appreciated the honesty in the meetings and recognized that, while the problems they face are large, the open and honest reflections enabled her to relax and feel fortified to move towards solutions. Another member said the discussions were helping everyone dig deeper into what was necessary to have an effective reopening. A new idea emerged as the focus of their work with students: How to help students become self-directed learners. This idea went considerably beyond how to simply help students re-enter school. "How do we do that?" someone asked. One teacher shared that if the group was going to work on this, they would not get it right quickly. It would take a lot of trial and error. Someone else noted that the faculty was stressed, and the time was not optimal to work on new approaches. The union representative shared it would be important to understand the needs of the faculty before they can serve the needs of students saying, "If we want to provide a supportive and engaging reopening for the students, we first have to do that for our colleagues." Shared silence indicated profound understanding.

Principal Jones interjected and suggested that perhaps they need to think about ways they can practice the very things they want for students with the faculty first. There was a lot of head nodding. Someone then asked what would that look like? The principal acknowledged it was an important question and one that perhaps should be the focus of the next faculty meeting. He asked everyone on the team to "turn and talk to a partner for 10 minutes." When the group reassembled and shared their thinking, it became clear the group's focus centered on this aspect of the reopening: How can we understand where each of our staff members is when they arrive back at school? How can we learn how they are doing emotionally? What surprised them about their spring experience? What did they learn about themselves and their students? How could they have been better supported?

The thinking that emerged from the group was it was important to first create a supportive climate for returning staff before engaging in new professional development. They realized they could not add one more thing to the overflowing plates of stressed teachers. They decided to first ask how teachers were doing and listen to them describe how their experiences at home and online had been. Someone noted this paralleled what teaches needed to do with returning students—establishing strong relationships before diving into new learning.

Meeting 5: Narrowing the Focus, Inviting Feedback

The participants felt good about the shift in focus (i.e., starting with staff) that occurred at the last meeting. Principal Jones asked if they would be willing to take on this area of focus and brainstorm possible approaches. He said that, if it worked, the group could divide up the additional areas and work in small teams to develop ideas for presentation at an upcoming faculty meeting.

The group decided to focus on the following: Prepare for a second quarantine by building on what we learned from our first quarantine. What worked? What do we want to do the same? What do we want to do differently? Their reasoning was that this learning was fresh in their minds and that will enable them to prepare for what many think will be an inevitable return to quarantine if a second round of the virus hits during the late fall or early winter.

The Faculty Meeting (Virtual)

The faculty meeting was led by educators from the team. Principal Jones noted that they seemed confident and excited to share their learning and insights with the larger group. They shared how group deliberations led to a shift in thinking and the realization that in order to better serve students, they had to first improve their understanding of the challenges, needs, and emotions of staff. Providing adults a sense of belonging and emotional support would ultimately lead to better support for the students. Though the Zoom meeting, one could see multiple heads nodding. A veteran teacher spoke up and acknowledged how powerful this was to hear from the team. She went on to say that during COVID-19 school closures and subsequent remote learning months in the spring, she felt isolated and that no one really understood what she was experiencing as a single mom who had to watch her own children while trying to teach her students. She added that having the administration understand and support the special circumstances she faced would energize her to do the same for her students.

Authors' Note

While the above is not the totality of the work of this team, we hope the vignette illustrates how paying attention to the framework can empower a group to gain important and vital insights into the roots of complex issues. Once the problem is understood at a deep level, appropriate strategies can be developed to address the underlying factors at the root of the problem. If the team had not realized a successful reopening must begin with addressing the needs of the staff, they more than likely would have jumped to a list of things to do for students. The problem with that approach, although logical, is that faculty deliver services and approaches to students. Without their readiness to do so, students are not well served. The vignette leaves out what steps the group recommended for the orientation of staff. Following our framework, whatever steps emerged from the group would have represented "small experiments," and data would need to be collected to see which approaches support the needs of the staff. It is this cycle of focusing first on the diagnosis and then moving to a series of experimental strategies that represent two key ideas of our framework.

We strongly believe our framework can be utilized by school leaders regardless of the student population they serve and the geography of their district. The implementation guidelines are intentionally flexible, allowing the framework to be implemented in coordination with existing practices present within school communities. Consistent with our recommendations to others, we believe that our framework should evolve over time to reflect stories of success and failure from school leaders on the front lines. To do so, we remain actively involved in schools directly and through ongoing consultations, and we look forward to continuing our data collection efforts to improve our framework. Lastly, we welcome and would greatly appreciate hearing from others who are willing to share their accomplishments and frustrations related to introducing our framework to their schools.

Reference

Schwarz, R. M. (2016). *The skilled facilitator: A comprehensive resource for consultants, facilitators, coaches, and trainers* (3rd ed.). Jossey-Bass.

Made in the USA
Middletown, DE
21 April 2021